Rooms of Their Own

Rooms of Their Own

Where Great Writers Write

Alex Johnson

Illustrations by James Oses

F

FRANCES
LINCOLN

Contents

Introduction

'Writers stamp themselves upon their possessions more indelibly than other people, making the table, the chair, the curtain, the carpet into their own image.'

Virginia Woolf, *Great Men's Houses* (1911)

Writers like ceremonies. Freshly sharpening a box of pencils every morning. Slurping a vast amount of coffee throughout the day. Or, in Gertrude Stein's case (see page 152), tracking down a docile cow for inspiration. But perhaps the most important of all is the commute, the ritual of going to a special place to write.

During lockdown, a lot of people discovered that what they really needed was a distinct space in which to work. Or, as Virginia Woolf famously put it in a lecture in 1929, 'a room of one's own'. For writers, somewhere private, quiet-ish and comfortable is particularly important.

These are fascinating spaces and we flock to see where Thomas Hardy created *Tess of the d'Urbervilles* and where J.K. Rowling conjured up Harry Potter. Indeed, literary tourism has a history stretching back 200 years, and writers themselves are also intrigued by other writers' rooms. Alfred Lord Tennyson visited Goethe's

home in Weimar, Germany, in 1865, and was fascinated by the German writer's 'sacred study'. As Hallam Tennyson revealed in his 1897 biography of his Poet Laureate father:

One cannot explain in words the awe and sadness with which this low dark room filled A. The study is narrow, and in proportion long. In the middle was a table with a cushion on it where Goethe would lean his arms, and a chair with a cushion where he sometimes sat, but his habit was to pace up and down and dictate to his secretary. On one side of the room was a bookcase about two-thirds up the wall, with boxes for his manuscripts. There were also visiting cards, strung like bills together, and Goethe's old, empty, wine bottles, in which the wine had left patterns like frost patterns. On the other side of the room was a calendar of things that had struck him in newspapers.

As Tennyson found, there is something fascinating to be experienced in the room where it happened, the views a favoured writer looked out on, the chairs they rested in, the atmosphere they created that in turn helped them create. These places offer the curious traveller more than just a peek into their owners' interior design tastes, they offer a biographical behind-the-scenes insight into what was deeply significant for them in their most personal space. Elsewhere in the same essay quoted at the start of this introduction, Virginia Woolf suggests that homes and their rooms make a significant impact on their owners' personalities, and that an hour in a house can be more revealing than a row of biographies.

Visiting these properties give us the opportunity to be a part of these writers' lives, take a look at the books on their shelves, relax at the familiar amount of clutter on their desks. If it's interesting to take a close look at a friend's house, how much more so is sitting on the chair in the room where James Bond came alive. These objects and spaces were witnesses

to something truly remarkable. You can wander through a writer's past as well as their space, and get a feeling about how they operated in the real world, and empathize with their messy desks or annoyingly creaky doors. We can get close to their minds, closer to understanding how their rooms and habits influenced their work. I remember the first time I stood outside George Bernard Shaw's revolving garden hut, and felt that I had somehow entered his extraordinary writing story (and I still feel the same every time I return each year).

It's not just private residences that provide perfect writing spaces. Libraries have been the thinking and researching spaces of writers for centuries. Chetham's in Manchester still reverently looks after the desk and alcove where Friedrich Engels and Karl Marx worked together in 1845, and Marx's daughter Eleanor made the first English translation of *Madame Bovary* during her visits to the British Museum Reading Room. Although not so many books are actually written in libraries, *Fahrenheit 451* by Ray Bradbury is among them.

And might some of the magic rub off? Brilliant people tackled the same

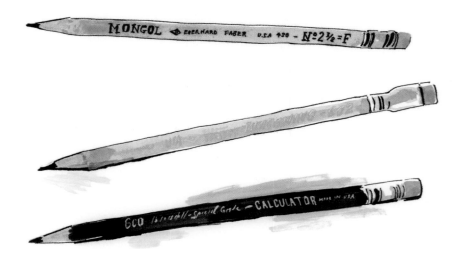

challenges that face us, and if writers within these walls (or in D.H. Lawrence's case, under these trees – see page 98) can develop successful creative ceremonies, perhaps we can adopt some to aid our own creativity? Though perhaps not those of German poet Friedrich von Schiller, who believed he could only write well when he could smell rotting apples, so kept a selection in his desk drawer.

So are there any truths universally acknowledged that we can learn from the places where great writers write? Although every writer has their own particular foibles and requirements, three elements appear especially important.

Firstly, whether it's a hut, a bedroom, a library or a car, writers like to establish a writing space that is at least partially protected from interruptions (although E.B. White also pointed out that there are *always* distractions because life is full of distractions – see page 172). Some, like Jonathan Franzen, simply remove all internet connections; others, like Maya Angelou (see page 14), get right away from their homes to anonymous writing 'safe houses' – in her case, undisclosed hotels.

This brings us on to the next point: the importance of making the best of what's available to you. Anthony Trollope produced most of *Barchester Towers* on the train during his work commute, writing in pencil on a home-made lapdesk, which he said he found just as convenient as a traditional one. A writing shed might be your ultimate retreat, but Louisa May Alcott managed to produce *Little Women* on a small but functional drop-down shelf her father knocked up in her bedroom.

Finally, wherever you write, try and do it in the morning. Even those writers who had a reputation for late late nights, and were by no stretch of the imagination 'morning people', often made sure they got in their daily session before lunch.

This is a book about all these people and all these rooms. Rooms that tell stories.

Isabel Allende
Making a date with a book

Writing studio, San Rafael, California

Isabel Allende (1942–) produced her first book – *The House of the Spirits* – on a typewriter in the kitchen of her flat in Caracas, to where she had fled following the military coup in her home country of Chile. She wrote mostly late in the evenings after working during the day and after cooking dinner. Subsequent books were written in a repurposed closet, coffee shops and in cars, but in 2001 she built a new home in San Rafael, California, overlooking San Franciso Bay. In the back garden she also built herself her *casita* (little house), which was initially planned as a pool house with its own bathroom, before it became her full-time writing studio for her next dozen books until her divorce and the sale of the property in 2016.

The *casita* was mainly a writing room, and nobody was allowed in, not even to clean – she described it as her 'sacred' space, and her 30-second commute to work as a journey to another world. Throughout her writing sessions, she kept interruptions to a minimum, since there was no phone or internet installed, to ensure a silent atmosphere for concentration, which she has likened to meditating. One exception to her 'no visitors' rule was its use as the regular meeting place for Allende's long-standing all-female prayer group, the Sisters of Perpetual Disorder, who have met fortnightly for decades for confidential discussion and mutual support.

It was also filled with meaningful objects, among them boxes of beads. Allende is a keen jewellery maker and uses beading to fend off tiredness and to clear her mind when writing or if she finds the words have temporarily stopped flowing. Elsewhere were the two rag dolls she made for her daughter Paula while she was pregnant with her, and whose tragically early death she chronicled in the 1994 memoir of the same name. One of Paula's white baby shoes was also always on display, as was a photograph

of her signing her wedding certificate. There were also decades of letters from her mother, stored away in a wardrobe. She felt that these, the photos and the evidence of her work, were a great support while she wrote.

The number of books in the room was fairly restrained: dictionaries on the desk and a first edition of each of her books on her bookshelves, including one in every language in which it has been printed. There were also the collected works of Chilean poet and politican Pablo Neruda and a copy of Shakespeare's works in Spanish, a present from her grandfather.

Allende starts every new novel on 8 January, what she calls her 'sacred day', after the letter she wrote on that day to her dying grandfather evolved into *The House of the Spirits* (she kept the typewriter she used to write it on her desk as a momento though she now writes with a computer). On this day, she makes an early start, and after walking her dogs and making time for

meditation, she has a cup of tea. She burns sage and candles to ask Paula's spirit and other ancestral muses to help her with the new book and gets underway (the previous day she cleans everything unconnected to the new book out of sight and donates all the books she has used to research the previous book to a charity in order to provide a clean palette for the new work).

As she progresses, she is at her desk every day except Sunday from 8.30 a.m. – after she has walked the dog, exercised and meditated – and writes until 7 p.m. with an afternoon break for a walk. This routine continues until she has completed her first draft, usually around May.

New Year's writing resolutions

Just like everybody else, writers make their own January promises to themselves to do better in the coming twelve months. Indeed, Samuel Pepys started his famous diary on 1 January 1660, which looks suspiciously like a New Year's resolution in itself – he used to write out what he called his 'vows' in a smaller book and take them with him as an encouragement. Though he did well with the diary, he was not so successful with other vows, including this one from 31 December 1661: 'I have newly taken a solemn oath about abstaining from plays and wine.'

In 1753, Samuel Johnson also promised himself in his annual New Year's prayer 'to keep a journal', in addition to his normal self-flagellatory remarks about how poorly he felt he had behaved in the previous twelve months.

Some writers were very specific. In January 1931, Virginia Woolf promised herself 'to make a good job of *The Waves*' and, more generally, 'sometimes to read, sometimes not to read', which is one everybody can keep. In 1986, Stephen King, smarting from criticisms about his latest novel (which ran to more than 1,100 pages), said he made his first New Year's resolution in a decade. 'Never,' he said, 'write anything bigger than your own head.'

Christopher Isherwood noted down many resolutions in his diaries, mostly encouraging himself to work faster and be less idle. But writers are only human and not all resolutions are kept despite the best intentions. On 1 January 1852, poet Robert Browning resolved to write a poem a day. He only lasted until 4 January.

Writing is, of course, not always uppermost in writers' minds as the new year changes. In 1905, P.G. Wodehouse's resolution was to learn to play the banjo.

Maya Angelou
Inspiration in a hotel room

Various hotels, including those in Winston-Salem, North Carolina

One of the most comfortable ways of avoiding the distractions of home life when writing is to check into a hotel.

Ernest Hemingway found Room 551 in the Hotel Ambos Mundos in Havana sufficiently inspiring to write parts of *For Whom the Bell Tolls* and *Death in the Afternoon*, and the room has since become a tiny museum in his honour. As the Savoy hotel in London's writer-in-residence in 2002, Fay Weldon was given a £350-a-night room in which to put pen to paper. And a Who's Who of writers chose the Chelsea Hotel in New York, including Jack Kerouac, William S. Burroughs and Arthur C. Clarke, who produced the screenplay for *2001: A Space Odyssey* in Room 1008.

Maya Angelou's (1928–2014) working routine was to wake early and head to a hotel room near her home, which she rented by the month. She chose fairly spartan surroundings: small rooms with nothing more than a bed and perhaps a basin and with the hotel paintings removed. The only things she brought with her from home were a bottle of sherry for occasional nips (usually at elevenses), a deck of cards, a copy of the King James Bible and a dictionary, sometimes a thesaurus and crossword puzzles. Work started around 6.30 a.m.

Angelou kept the identity of these hotels a secret and relied upon loyal hotel staff to keep interruptions to a minimum (they came in only to empty the wastebasket and change the sheets) and feign ignorance when people asked if she were in the building. Her home in later years was Winston-Salem in North Carolina, and she probably used the city's Historic Brookstown Inn and Kimpton Cardinal Hotel.

In the hotel room, she would lie on the bed to write in longhand on yellow legal pads, returning home to work in the afternoon for a break and a shower. Here she would edit in the early evening using a typewriter, latterly a 1980s Adler Meteor 12.

Comfort without distraction was the key to Angelou's writing routine.

Margaret Atwood
Who needs a writing room anyway?

Anywhere

Not all writers require a specific writing room in which to work, or have agonizingly precise daily writing routines. Canadian novelist and poet Margaret Atwood (1939–), author of *The Testaments* and *Oryx and Crake*, is among those who take quite a relaxed approach to the nuts and bolts of their writing process.

For a start, she does not write every day. Nor does she go through a series of rituals beforehand. And when she feels the writing has come to a stop, she simply goes and does something else to clear her mind, especially if it is something repetitive and entirely unconnected to writing. Although Atwood has no set routine, she writes in longhand first, then transcribes a couple of dozen pages on her computer (in her early days as a novelist she used a typewriter) before returning to pen and paper. She calls this technique her 'rolling barrage' approach, a reference to an artillery tactic used during the First World War. This was how she wrote her modern classic *The Handmaid's Tale*, using a large rented German manual typewriter, while she was living in West Berlin for a year in 1984, before the Wall came down.

> *She does not write every day. Nor does she go through a series of rituals beforehand. And when she feels the writing has come to a stop, she simply goes and does something else to clear her mind.*

Her daily wordcount goal is in the 1,000–2,000 ballpark, working on a new work for a couple of hours a day at the beginning, but gradually increasing the hours as she reaches the end. In her twenties, when she had various part-time jobs, she often wrote at night, but as she became more successful, she moved to writing in the morning and then from 10 a.m. to 4 p.m. while her daughter was at school.

Atwood is as happy writing in a plane – or a coffee shop – as at a desk.

Like other busy writers who work on the move, Atwood finds it possible to work in varied locations, from hotel rooms and coffee shops to aeroplanes. 'I don't really have a writing space,' she says, although she prefers a window wherever possible and does have a study where she often works. Here, she has a couple of computers: on one desk, one with an internet connection (she likes Twitter, though she restricts her use to about ten minutes a day to prevent her being overly distracted – see Zadie Smith, page 146); and another on a second desk, which is deliberately not hooked up to the web. Atwood is certainly no technophobe, however, and came up with the idea of the first remote document-signing device, the Long Pen, in 2004.

As well as using her desks, she also writes lying down or in a semi-crouching position. One thing she doesn't do is write with music in the background.

Atwood is a keen user of notebooks and yellow legal pads, ideally with margins and thickly spaced lines to leave room for annotations. Her rule here is that if she buys too nice a notebook, then she feels bad about defacing it. As well as carrying notebooks with her on the move, she also keeps one by her bedside. She does admit to having plenty of pens on her desk, including ones she has converted into writing implements from feathers she has collected. The study also contains plenty

of books, but none of what she describes as 'magical objects' to inspire her.

There is one writerly tradition to which she does hold. Coffee plays a big part in her working day – she worked in a coffee shop before her novels propelled her to fame – and has even partnered with Canadian coffee shop chain Balzac's to produce her own eponymous medium roast blend ('a mild and gracious backdrop allowing a supple caramel finish'). It is certified as bird-friendly as Atwood is a keen environmentalist and has a long-standing connection with bird conservation.

Lying down

Writing lying down or in bed is a common part of many writers' routines. There is even some research that suggests horizontal working is more conducive to creative problem solving than remaining upright. Recumbent office desks are also on the rise.

For some writers, it is only part of their routine. Russian-American novelist Vladimir Nabokov spent a lot of time writing in bed as a young man, but then moderated the habit to include a standing desk and an armchair. Eccentric English poet Edith Sitwell is said to have prepared for a day's writing, usually surrounded by various lined notebooks, by contemplating her work ahead from the comfort of an open coffin (maybe take this with a large pinch of salt). And lying on his stomach was James Joyce's preferred method while writing in large blue pencil and wearing a white coat, to help deal with his worsening eyesight.

But the most committed to non-verticality was Truman Capote, who once described himself as a 'completely horizontal author'. He wrote longhand in this ideal position and kept cigarettes and coffee to hand, moving on to mint tea, sherry and then martinis as the day progressed.

W.H. Auden
A room of genius and squalor

Flat, New York; attic, Kirchstetten, Austria

'Be regular and orderly in your life,' French novelist Gustave Flaubert is reputed to have said, 'so that you may be violent and original in your work.' While the work of English poet W.H. (Wystan Hugh) Auden (1907–73) was certainly original, it's hard to level the charge of an orderly writing room against him.

Auden said he believed that routine was a sign of ambition, and wrote every morning from 6 a.m. after having a coffee and a look at a crossword, before knocking off around noon. After half an hour for lunch, he would return to work in the afternoon but stopped before evening. During working hours he discouraged any visitors. Auden wrote early drafts in notebooks, starting on the right-hand page then revising on the left-hand one, in a longhand compared by Geoffrey Grigson, the editor of poetry magazine *New Verse*, as 'writing an airborne daddy-long-legs might have managed'. Auden memorably suggested that people relish the look of their own handwriting in the same way that they 'enjoy the smell of their own farts'. He then typed up the final work, although he claimed to loathe typewriters, as typed lines seemed 'so impersonal and hideous to look at'.

In general, he was punctual in his habits and excellent at meeting deadlines, checking his watch with the same regularity as some people check their social media. And his output of poems – including 'Funeral Blues' ('Stop all the clocks') and 'Night Mail' – and opera libretti, showed his formal mastery of the written word. But he did it all in the most appalling mess.

Auden led an itinerant life, usually summering in Europe and spending the rest of the year in New York, particularly in a flat on the Lower East Side, which he called 'my N.Y. nest', but which political theorist Hannah Arendt called his 'slum apartment', and artist Margaret Gardiner called a 'brownish cavern'. Here, he wrote on a small table in a little room with a

Auden was no tidier in his rural Austrian home than he was in his New York 'nest'.

green marbled fireplace and built-in bookshelves. He always kept the curtains closed.

His friend the American poet Charles Miller politely characterized this 'Auden-scape' in his 1983 memoir *Auden: An American Friendship* as 'cluttered' but his description of the main table, covered in books, magazines, half-drunk 'scummed over' coffee cups, bits of bread, a large dish of cigarette butts and olive stones, is distinctly unappealing. Cutlery and dinner plates were poorly cleaned. The atmosphere reeked of nicotine and stale coffee. Gardiner said even the air had the feeling of brownness about it. His friend Igor Stravinsky called him 'the dirtiest man I have ever liked'. Auden said he hated living in squalor 'but I can't do the work I want to do and live any other way'.

On top of all this, he smoked heavily and took large and regular doses of the amphetamine Benzedrine to help get him going first thing in the morning (what he called a 'labour-saving device'). During the day he moved on to large amounts of alcohol, with cocktails at 5 p.m., and used sedatives to go to sleep at night (with a bottle of vodka next to his bed in case he woke up and needed a nip in the small hours). He called this arrangement his 'chemical life'.

Auden replicated this domestic squalor at the farmhouse he bought in Kirchstetten, Austria, in 1958, his attic writing study there immortalized in his 1965 *Thanksgiving for a Habitat* poem sequence in 'The Cave of Making' and 'Up There'. This has been partly turned into an Auden museum and his writing room in the eaves is kept largely as it was in Auden's day (though it has been tidied up), with his wooden writing desk by the window, bookshelves full of his favourite Penguin crime novels, Olivetti typewriter, ashtray and slippers.

> *The atmosphere reeked of nicotine and stale coffee. Gardiner said even the air had the feeling of brownness about it. His friend Igor Stravinsky called him 'the dirtiest man I have ever liked'.*

Jane Austen
The consequence of moving writing rooms

Dining parlour, Chawton, Hampshire

Anyone who has moved home knows how disorienting it can be, and it certainly had a profound effect on English novelist Jane Austen (1775–1817).

Austen was very happy and productive while living in the family home in Steventon, Hampshire. She wrote on a portable mahogany writing box given to her by her father in 1794 as a birthday present. When opened, it offered a sloping writing surface as well as special compartments for paper and ink plus a lockable drawer, and it was probably on this that she produced early versions of *Pride and Prejudice*, *Sense and Sensibility* and *Northanger Abbey*. It was one of her most treasured possessions and she kept her spectacles in it. In a 1798 letter to her sister Cassandra, she recounts her horror when it was nearly accidentally shipped off to the West Indies.

Initially, Austen wrote on small slips of paper that fitted easily into her writing box. As her style developed, her manuscripts were mostly written on sixteen-page 'booklets', which were assembled inside one another to make fatter books.

From 1809, Austen was also very happy and productive while living in the family home in Chawton, Hampshire. Here, she wrote every day in the dining parlour on a tiny twelve-sided walnut table – a far simpler object than the writing box and certainly not built as a writing desk. This stood close to the window where the light was best, with a view of the road through the village. This table is on display in what is now a museum. It is so small, in fact, that it seems likely she also wrote elsewhere in the house, although she had no dedicated writing room. She worked with a quill and home-made oak apple/iron-gall ink, revising her Steventon novels and then going on to write *Mansfield Park*, *Emma* and *Persuasion*. One story about her writing room routine, which originated from her nephew

Austen wrote privately in a very public domestic setting of her home.

James Edward Austen-Leigh's memoir of her, is that she liked to keep her writing a secret and a creaking door alerted her to people coming into the room. 'She was careful that her occupation should not be suspected by servants or visitors, or any persons beyond her own family party,' he wrote. Her writing routine was also largely free from domestic chores, other than making morning tea.

But in the half-dozen years between Steventon and Chawton, during which she lived in Bath, Austen wrote very little indeed, and abandoned her unfinished novel, *The Watsons*. The reasons are not entirely clear, and while she does occasionally write somewhat dismissively of Bath in her letters, she does not seem to have been

She worked with a quill and home-made oak apple/iron-gall ink, revising her Steventon novels and then going on to write Mansfield Park, Emma *and* Persuasion.

terribly miserable either. Certainly, she was very busy socially and also did a lot of travelling, which would have got in the way of writing. Other suggestions include depression; she most definitely did not want to move from Steventon and the decision was very much sprung upon her by her parents. Her nephew James suggested that 'The loss of their first home is generally a great grief to young persons of strong feeling' and that it made her 'exceedingly unhappy'. Whatever combination of all these factors, moving to Bath was more than moving house; it ripped Austen away from her writing routine and caused a significant writer's block.

Austen's sloping writing desk, now part of the British Library's collection.

James Baldwin
Writing at night

Café de Flore, Paris; study, Saint-Paul de Vence, Provence, France

American novelist and essayist James Baldwin (1924–87) is among the many writers who produced some of their finest work outside their home country. He moved to France in 1948 where he lived in Paris and the picturesque village of Saint-Paul de Vence in Provence, and spent most of the 1960s in Turkey, continuing to write about America (though he disliked the badge he was sometimes given as an 'expatriate' or 'self-exiled' writer). One thing that was constant throughout his career was that he wrote almost exclusively at night, starting after dinner and finishing around 4 a.m.

This was a habit that was forced upon him as a teenager living in New York, when he looked after his younger siblings and worked during the day, leaving him only the night for writing. He continued the routine as an adult because he said it was the only time he could be alone.

In Paris, Baldwin wrote his first novel, the semi-autobiographical *Go Tell It on the Mountain* (1953), at the Café de Flore in Paris. 'The moment I began living in French hotels I understood the necessity of French cafés,' he wrote in his essay 'Equal in Paris', from his collection *Notes of a Native Son* (1955). 'This made it rather difficult to look me up, for as soon as I was out of bed I hopefully took notebook and fountain pen off to the upstairs room of the Flore, where I consumed rather a lot of coffee and, as evening approached, rather a lot of alcohol, but did not get much writing done.'

For the last decade and a half of his life he wrote in his home overlooking the Mediterranean in the south of France, a twelve-room, 300-year-old stone former farmhouse that became known locally as Chez Baldwin. This inspired his work, including his final unpublished play *The Welcome Table*, a reference to the round table on his stone patio, where he entertained many

Baldwin was much happier writing (and living) in Paris than in America.

famous writers such as Maya Angelou and Toni Morrison, as well as musicians including Miles Davis, Josephine Baker and Nina Simone. After his night-time writing sessions, he always got up at noon to greet these guests.

While his home was something of a social whirl for international visitors, at night Baldwin would work in his living quarters located on the bottom level at the back of the house, which included a small kitchen, bathroom and his study, the same space in which the French artist Georges Braque had painted. Baldwin's protégé Cecil Brown described the room as smelling of whisky and cigarettes, with an open fireplace and a red carpet. Baldwin worked at a large table, sometimes writing on blank white pads but preferring to use a typewriter. He owned several of these over his lifetime, including an Adler Gabriele 35, a Smith-Corona Coronamatic 2200 and an Olympia SM7.

During breaks from his work, he would relax at the table on the stone patio. He described it as 'an island of silence and peace' in a 1987 article for *Architectural Digest* magazine.

He also described his writing room as his 'dungeon' and 'torture chamber' in a letter to his brother David in 1975. Baldwin admitted that he found the energy required for the writing process increasingly difficult to keep up as he got older, and called his career a terrible way to make a living. Nevertheless, he was a conscientious and hugely industrious writer who wrote prolifically at Saint-Paul de Vence, including his collection of non-fiction *No Name in the Street* (1972), the novel *If Beale Street Could Talk* (1974) and his only collection of poems, *Jimmy's Blues* (1983).

Sadly, Chez Baldwin will never be established as a writer's house museum or even the retreat for African diaspora writers he hoped it might become. After his death it fell into disrepair and, despite various fundraising campaigns, it was demolished to make way for a new luxury housing development.

Writing in watering holes

Baldwin is certainly not the only writer to find inspiration in watering holes. Fellow frequenters of the Café de Flore in Paris, Jean-Paul Sartre and Simone de Beauvoir often settled in at 9 a.m. and, with a two-hour break for lunch at midday, worked through until 8 p.m., talking, writing and philosophizing with friends. O. Henry (real name William Porter) wrote his famous short story 'The Gift of the Magi' in 1905 in Pete's Tavern in New York, and Malcolm 'Tipping Point' Gladwell has written about how he finds coffee shops inspirational places for thinking about his writing ideas. In Spain, *tertulias* – a kind of semi-formal literary salon – have been held for hundreds of years in numerous bars and cafés, such as the Café Gijón in Madrid. Novelist and literary critic Ford Madox Ford described a café as 'a serious place where serious people discussing serious subjects mould civilizations', and Sartre mentions in his *War Diaries* that cafés provided him with everything he needed to write: coffee, tobacco, a table and pens.

Honoré de Balzac
Coffee and strange hours

Study, Paris; bedroom, Château de Saché, Tours, France

From Voltaire and Jonathan Swift to Gustave Flaubert and Terry Pratchett, coffee has for centuries been as much a necessity for writers as paper. It was certainly true for French novelist Honoré de Balzac (1799–1850). 'Coffee is a great power in my life.' he wrote in his treatise 'The Pleasures and Pains of Coffee', marvelling at how it not only stimulates the mind but puts sleep to flight.

It was the most essential thing to be found in his writing rooms and he drank vast quantities of it, a blend of three different beans – Bourbon, Martinique and Mocha – which he always made himself. It's hard to estimate exactly how much he consumed – one guess is up to fifty cups a day – not least because he probably drank from a small demitasse rather than a mug. When it seemed not to be having the desired effect, he simply ate ground coffee beans neat, though he did acknowledge this to be a 'horrible, rather brutal method', which he compared to the battalions of an army gearing up for battle.

The tremendous flood of caffeine helped him power through his strange choice of working hours. As a young man, Balzac specifically said that he chose to be a writer over a lawyer because he could not stand the idea of 'eating, drinking and sleeping at fixed hours'. In a letter to his friend and later wife Eveline Hańska, he describes his work routine – waking up at midnight to write for eight hours, then fifteen minutes for lunch followed by five more hours of work, before dinner and bed. Sometimes he threw in a nap before breakfast. Balzac once claimed that he survived a forty-eight-hour intensive writing session on a mere three hours sleep. However, he realized this was not conducive to a healthy life. 'I'm not living,' he admitted. 'I'm wearing myself out ... driven by the terrible demon of work.'

For much of the 1840s, this work was done in the top-floor study of his home in the 16th arrondissement of Paris, which is

Coffee, 2 a.m. starts and a raven's feather quill pen were elements of Balzac's writing sessions.

now the Maison de Balzac. On display here is his surprisingly small white porcelain coffee pot, with amaranth purple trim bearing his monogram. The curtains were usually closed and his light came from two four-branched candlesticks of unpolished bronze.

Balzac sat on a tapestry-covered chair with long curling arms, writing on a small wooden table, which he always took with him when he moved house. It was covered in green baize, and he said it had seen 'all of my misery' as well as being almost worn away by his arm rubbing across it as he wrote. The table had a low cross-bar, on which he appears not to have rested his feet regularly, since it is still in good condition. Among the many things he worked on here was his multi-volume novel series, *La Comédie humaine*.

While he wrote he wore red slippers and a monk-like white cotton robe tied around his stomach with a Venetian gold chain. From the chain hung a paper-knife, scissors and a gold penknife. He wrote using a raven's feather quill pen on paper with a slightly blue-ish tinge to avoid tiring his eyes.

Although Balzac's other Parisian homes are no longer standing, he also wrote regularly at the Château de Saché near Tours, owned by his friend Jean de Margonne and now the Musée Balzac. When he was not writing in the second-floor bedroom, he enjoyed the calm and fresh air on long walks here. A contemporary account describes his working day as always starting at 2 a.m. (woken up by an alarm clock), with coffee and toast, then writing in bed on a specially adapted table until 5 p.m., when he broke for dinner and then retired to bed at 10 p.m.

Writers and their chairs

Writers working away for hours at a time need a comfortable chair. Prolific German playwright, poet and novelist Johann von Goethe was well aware of the advantages of a healthy ergonomic writing environment. He usually wrote at a standing desk, but when he became tired, instead of throwing himself into a soft armchair, he perched on a high wooden stool called a *sitzbock*. Also known as a 'donkey', it looks like a cross between a small pommel horse and an upholstered saddle for riding horses, with four sloping legs. It's more for perching on, half-standing, allowing the back muscles to relax while keeping the spine upright.

Both Mark Twain and Charles Dickens liked chairs with cane seating. Dickens in particular was very keen on his because he suffered from an anal fistula and he thought the cane provided plenty of soothing air around his bottom. He wrote to his friend, the journalist and printer Francis Dalziel Finlay, who had also undergone an operation for the condition: 'You know by this time, I may assume, the importance of always using an open-work cane chair? I can testify that there is nothing quite like it. Even in this episodical hotel-life, I invariably have my cane chair brought from a bedroom.'

The chair on which J.K. Rowling drafted parts of *Harry Potter and the Philosopher's Stone* (1997) and *Harry Potter and the Chamber of Secrets* (1998) was not at all fancy. It was a simple oak dining-room chair with a red thistle decoration dating from the 1930s. After *Goblet of Fire* came out in 2000 she donated it to a charity auction, having repainted it with an inscription around its frame: 'You may not find me pretty but don't judge on what you see. I wrote Harry Potter while sitting on this chair.' Rowling was given the chair for free in 1995 for her Edinburgh council flat. It sold at auction in 2016 for £278,000 along with a letter of provenance from Rowling, which stated 'My nostalgic side is quite sad to see it go, but my back isn't.'

Perhaps the Holy Grail of literary chairs is Shakespeare's. There are various contenders, including a carved oak one at the National Trust's property Anglesey Abbey in Cambridgeshire, although definite evidence is in slightly short supply.

Ray Bradbury
The lure of the basement

Basement, University of California's Powell Library, Los Angeles; home basement, Culver City, California

During the 1940s and early 1950s, American novelist and short story writer Ray Bradbury (1920–2012) usually wrote in the garages of his homes. The downside of this was that his young children used to come and ask him to play with them, which rather distracted him. In a bid to find a new writing room, he settled on the typing room in the basement of the University of California's Powell Library in Los Angeles.

Here, he discovered rows of Remington and Underwood typewriters, which could be rented out at ten cents per half hour, a ticking clock providing incentive to write speedily. Which he did, finishing the 25,000 words of the first draft of *Fahrenheit 451* in about nine days for what he estimated was $9.80.

To some extent he replicated that atmosphere in the home office of his house where he wrote in the basement. He surrounded himself with the creative detritus accumulated throughout his life, from ticket stubs to a globe of Mars presented to him by NASA. So in addition to his usual writing equipment (typewriters, never computers), there were piles of cheap pulp magazines, filing cabinets full of all his manuscripts and notes, as well as floor-to-ceiling bookshelves and his desk, above which he pinned a note that said 'Don't think'. He also hung many masks from the ceiling, placed a six-foot stuffed replica of the cartoon character Bullwinkle on a chair and covered an entire wall with a painting of Mr Electro from *Something Wicked This Way Comes*, which he wrote down there. Bradbury loved toys, and the office contained many which were Christmas presents to him from his wife, including model dinosaurs and tin robots.

The basement also featured props for dramatizations of his stories, among them a jar with a fake human head in it, from Alfred Hitchcock's version of his short story *The Jar*.

Bradbury worked surrounded by much-loved objects, from set props to ticket stubs.

The Brontës
Managing a co-working space

Dining/drawing room, Haworth, West Yorkshire

The concept of a writers' room – somewhere a group of writers on a television series comes together to forge ongoing storylines – is a familiar one in the twenty-first century. But 150 years ago the Brontë sisters were pioneering a very similar approach.

The three sisters, and their brother Branwell, had an intense sibling relationship, together charting their imaginary worlds of Angria and Gondal, writing and producing tiny books about these lands at their home in Haworth Parsonage, and going on to publish their first book of poems together. Charlotte's biographer, the novelist Elizabeth Gaskell, described how they worked.

The sisters retained the old habit, which was begun in their aunt's life-time, of putting away their work at nine o'clock, and beginning their study, pacing up and down the sitting room. At this time, they talked over the stories they were engaged upon, and described their plots. Once or twice a week, each read to the others what she had written, and heard what they had to say about it. Charlotte told me that the remarks made had seldom any effect in inducing her to alter her work, so possessed was she with the feeling that she had described reality; but the readings were of great and stirring interest to all, taking them out of the gnawing pressure of daily-recurring cares, and setting them in a free place.

They sewed and wrote and chatted about their writings together in this room, variously known as the dining room, drawing room or parlour. Charlotte's *Jane Eyre*, Emily's *Wuthering Heights* and Anne's *Agnes Grey* were all written on the family's mahogany drop-leaf dining table here, on display in the parsonage today with its ink blots, candle burn in the centre and small letter 'E' carved into its top.

The space at home where the Brontë sisters lived and wrote together.

Charlotte

Anne

Emily

When Gaskell visited in September 1853, she commented on how clean and neat it was, 'the perfection of warmth, snugness and comfort, crimson predominating in the furniture ... simple, good, sufficient for every possible reasonable want'. This visit came after the success of *Jane Eyre*, so Charlotte had recently received the funds to make the room bigger and buy the red carpet and curtains, which Gaskell also remarked upon. Each sister had a portable – and lockable – rosewood desk with a velvet writing slope, which they called a 'desk box', with room for ink, stationery, pens and nibs, blotting paper and other small valuables. In the summer, they also wrote in the parsonage garden, carrying out small wooden stools and desks and sitting near the currant bushes.

> *Each sister had a portable rosewood desk with a velvet writing slope, which they called a 'desk box', with room for ink, stationery, pens and nibs, blotting paper and other small valuables.*

Of course, they did not always write together. Anne started her first novel in the early 1840s while working as a governess near York. Emily was more discreet about writing her poems as an adult, and was very angry when Charlotte came across and read them without permission. But for much of their lives they operated as a single collaborative entity: the Brontës.

The importance of their working relationship is clear from a letter Charlotte wrote about her last novel, *Villette*, to her publisher George Smith. 'How I have sometimes desponded and almost despaired because there was no one to whom to read a line – or of whom to ask a counsel,' she wrote. '*Jane Eyre* was not written under such circumstances, nor were two-thirds of *Shirley*.' The sisters had chatted about their writing and walked around the dining room table until 11 p.m. every night, and after Emily and Anne died, Charlotte continued the ritual alone. Her servant at the parsonage, Martha Brown, described how: 'My heart aches to hear Miss Brontë walking, walking on alone.' Charlotte lost not only her siblings but also the other members of her writers' room.

The sisters each had a 'desk box' on which to write.

Anton Chekhov
Rooms with inspirational views

Various studies, Melikhovo and Yalta, Russia

Russian short story genius and playwright Anton Chekhov (1860–1904) had several fairly conventional studies where he wrote and, while he was not fixated about maintaining the sanctity of his writing room, the placement of his desk was important.

Forty miles south of Moscow, at his country estate at Melikhovo, Chekhov lived in the one-storey main house with his sister and parents. Here, he placed the desk in his study by the window overlooking his beloved garden, apple trees and herb garden.

Interruptions to his work were frequent. He took it upon himself as a benevolent landlord to help deal with his tenants' cholera outbreaks and general health issues, doubling up his study as an informal doctor's surgery. Two years after he moved in, he built a small guest cottage in the cherry orchard close to the house, complete with terrace overlooking the garden and he wrote here in the upstairs room. This is where he finished his plays *The Seagull* (1895) and *Uncle Vanya* (1896). He put up a home-made sign outside which read: 'My house, where I began The Seagull.' While he wrote, Chekhov enjoyed coffee in the morning, and then a kind of soupy broth around midday. His study was nicely furnished with a writing desk, sofa, chairs and many paintings, photographs and prints hanging on the walls.

His friend, the Russian playwright Ignaty Potapenko, wrote that when guests were visiting, Chekhov spent all his time with them except for occasional moments when he nipped out to his study, wrote down whatever had just burst into his mind and then returned to be a good host.

But Chekhov's inspiration often came from outside the study. What sustained him and his writing was his garden. He read up voraciously on all aspects of horticulture, planting flowers, trees and vegetables, and working on the garden himself rather than

A keen horticulturalist as well as writer and doctor, Chekhov enjoyed the garden view from his desk.

relying on hired help. Indeed, he commented that if he couldn't work in the garden every day, he wouldn't be able to write.

'I think that if I wasn't a writer,' he said, 'I could be a gardener.' It was here where the author of *The Cherry Orchard* planted his own orchard of fifty trees, which in a sad example of life imitating art was cut down after he sold the estate in 1899.

Chekhov wrote his manuscripts using pen and ink, though used a pencil to write in his notebooks. These show what a central part his gardens played in his life, future projects and names of plants appearing throughout, as they also did in his letters to friends and family. Among the lists is one of every single species that he planted in his garden. This habit spread and the manuscript of *The Seagull* has lists of bulbs and the names of plants in its margins. As in many of this other works, flowers and gardens appear constantly in his characters' speeches. In *Uncle Vanya*, the doctor Astrov is a strong believer in the importance of forests as natural resources, while the threatened destruction of the fruit trees is the central plank of *The Cherry Orchard*.

He read up voraciously on all aspects of horticulture, planting flowers, trees and vegetables, and working on the garden himself rather than relying on hired help.

Following the triumph of *The Seagull*, Chekhov bought land and had a new house built on the edge of Yalta, a coastal resort on the Black Sea. Known as the White Dacha, it was here he wrote *Three Sisters* and *The Cherry Orchard*. Again, although he had a comfortable study with a large blue desk, patterned wallpaper and pictures (including one by his father and a landscape by the popular Russian artist Isaac Levitan), it was his garden and surroundings that provided him with comfort as his struggle with tuberculosis worsened. One of his most famous short stories, 'The Lady with the Dog', was inspired by the view from his study window of the local seafront. Yalta was a fashionable holiday retreat for the country's well-to-do, as well as infamous for its connection with extra-marital affairs, and this forms the basis of this story about infidelity.

'There is no easy road to successful authorship; it has to be earned by long & patient labor, many disappointments, uncertainties & trials.'

Louisa May Alcott

'The best time to plan a book is while you're doing the dishes.'

Agatha Christie

Agatha Christie
A steady table and a typewriter

Various rooms, including homes in London and Wallingford, Oxfordshire

The author of the world's most popular detective mysteries, indeed the best-selling novelist ever, remarked that she never had a particular room or place where she went to write. 'All I needed,' wrote Agatha Christie (1890–1976) in her 1977 *An Autobiography*, 'was a steady table and a typewriter.'

It's a nice phrase but only partly true, since she did have rooms at some of her homes in London where she sat down with her pen and typewriter, as well as at her home in Wallingford, Oxfordshire, where she lived for the second half of her life. So in her mews home at Cresswell Place – inspiration for her 1937 short story 'Murder in the Mews' – she undertook substantial work to add a slightly out of place, extra mini-storey to use specifically as a writing room.

At Sheffield Terrace, where she lived with her second husband, the archaeologist Max Mallowan, between 1934 and 1941, Christie certainly did have a dedicated writing room. It was here that she wrote *Death on the Nile*, *Murder in Mesopotamia* and some of *Murder on the Orient Express* (although the Pera Palace Hotel in Istanbul also claims that Room 411 was where she worked on the latter, and has turned it into something of a shrine to her).

She was keen that her room in Sheffield Terrace should be somewhere she could work without being disturbed, in particular a room without a telephone. Instead, she furnished it with a Steinway grand piano, what she described as a 'large, firm table' and a 'hard upright chair for typing', a comfortable sofa and an armchair to relax in. It was certainly better than her previous and smaller home in London in Campden Street (where she wrote the Miss Marple mystery *The Murder at the Vicarage*), which did not have room for a special study.

Writing rooms aside, Christie took the opportunity to plan her books and write anywhere, including a tent while she was

Christie could work anywhere, though favoured bathtimes as ideal moments for brainstorming plots.

accompanying her husband on his excavations in the Middle East. She said she often came up with ideas for books while having a bath and eating numerous apples – partly because it meant she was undisturbed – and, using her 'steady table' method, admitted that she found it as easy to work on her marble-topped bedroom washstand table and the dining-room table as at a desk.

Generally she started a new book in January and finished it around springtime, consulting the extensive notebooks in which she constantly logged her ideas. For a large part of her working life, she would work on two books simultaneously, which accounts for her huge output. Marketing played a key part in her success too, as from the late 1940s her latest book would be published in time for Christmas and promoted as a 'Christie for Christmas' tradition. Her preferred typewriter was a Remington Victor T – Christie experimented with dictating her stories to an assistant but found the process difficult and only used a dictaphone later in life when she broke her wrist.

The home most associated with Christie is Greenway House in Devon. Very lightly fictionalized, it is the house which is the centre of the action in her 1956 Poirot novel *Dead Man's Folly*. But Greenway was a holiday home and she didn't write here. However, her grandson Mathew Prichard has talked about how she tested out her mystery *A Pocket Full of Rye* on the family by reading chapters out loud to them and asking the family to deduce 'whodunnit'.

Colette
From a prison cell to a raft

Upstairs room, Besançon, France; flat, Paris

Most writers understandably make their writing room somewhere comfortable for work. But it is still perfectly possible to be both successful and prolific in less salubrious conditions. The Marquis de Sade's decade behind bars in the Bastille saw him complete *Justine* and *The 120 Days of Sodom*, while Oscar Wilde wrote *De Profundis* in Reading Gaol.

Sidonie-Gabrielle Colette (1873–1954), author of the Claudine series and *Gigi* and better known simply as Colette, found it hard to write and was adept at procrastinating, such as spending ages picking fleas off her bulldog Souci. 'To write is the joy and torment of the idle,' she wrote in her story *La Vagabonde*. Annoyed that she had produced very few pages at their country house in Besançon, France, Colette's husband Henry Gauthier-Villars, known as Willy, simply took her by the hand, threw her into an upstairs room and locked the door from the outside. He told her he would return four hours later and expected to see results.

Some critics have cast doubt on the truth of this story, at least to what extent Colette was complicit in her confinement. But in her autobiographic *Earthly Paradise* she says: 'A prison is indeed one of the best workshops ... I know what I am talking about: a real prison, the sound of the key turning in the lock and four hours claustration before I was free again.'

In her Paris flat in later life, suffering from arthritis, she wrapped herself in a blanket or fur rug and set up a lap table over her legs on which to write using a Mandarin Yellow Parker Duofold pen. Her bedside light was covered in a shade made from her favourite blue writing paper. Rather than calling this a prison, she described this final writing set-up as her 'raft'.

Colette enjoyed the comforts of writing in bed in later life.

Roald Dahl
A children's writer in a temple to childhood

Writing shed, Great Missenden, Buckinghamshire

Roald Dahl (1916–90) wrote about children for children and he did so surrounded by mementoes of childhood – mostly his own, his children's and his grandchildren's – in the brick writing hut at the bottom of his garden in Great Missenden, Buckinghamshire.

The hut was built by Dahl's friend, a local builder called Wally Saunders (later the inspiration for the BFG), and every last part – including the dust – moved into the Roald Dahl Museum and Story Centre in 2012. Inside is an old Parker Knoll armchair where Dahl sat, writing on a green baize-covered wooden board balanced across its arms. Everywhere there is the flotsam and jetsam of life, from his own hipbone to the ashtray filled with his old Marlboro cigarette butts and the untouched rubbish in his wastepaper bin.

He called it his 'little nest' and the layout has a feeling of a home-made cockpit about it. Dahl tucked himself tightly into position each morning, six yellow pencils in a jar beside him which he used to write on yellow American legal paper, a thermos flask of coffee and a very dangerous-looking heater, reachable without moving from his seat. Indeed, the hut is decorated with many reminders of his time as a pilot, including a picture of a Tiger Moth in which he learnt to fly while in the RAF in the Second World War, various models of Hurricanes (which he also piloted) and also of other planes, including a Gloster Gladiator, which is what he was flying when he crashed in the Libyan desert in 1940.

He allowed almost nobody in and told children they were banned because there were wolves inside. Yet it was a temple to childhood and Dahl remarked that: 'I can cut myself off there and within minutes become six and seven and eight again.'

As soon as he set himself down he was surrounded by images of children. The view to the right of his chair as he worked

Dahl's idiosyncratic workplace, now a popular feature at the museum dedicated to his life and work.

was filled with photos and memorabilia, all held in place by paperclips Dahl opened out and stuck into the hut's makeshift polystyrene insulation. Pride of place goes to family photographs, including one of Patricia Neal, his first wife, with their daughters Ophelia and Tessa; another of his son Theo and of his daughter Olivia, who died aged seven in 1962 from measles encephalitis. Dotted around are paintings by his granddaughter Sophie, aged four, and by his youngest daughter Lucy, as well as a photo of Dahl meeting young fans. There are also various postcards of Repton School, where he was a boarder. Elsewhere from his school days there is an old clothes brush with his name scratched into it, which he used to brush bits of dirt off his writing board each morning before he started work. Other odds and ends include a goodbye note from a young girl he met on holiday in France.

Although all his children are in evidence in the hut, it is Olivia whose image is prevalent. Opposite his chair is a pastel portrait of her by artist Amelia Shaw Hastings.

On the table by his chair is a photo of his grandson Luke's fourth birthday at Dahl's Gipsy House home in Buckinghamshire; a photo of him hugging Sophie; a rock veined with opal sent to him by a young boy fan in Australia; and a pinecone, a reminder of his happy childhood holidays in Norway.

Although all his children are in evidence in the hut, it is Olivia whose image is prevalent. Opposite his chair is a pastel portrait of her by artist Amelia Shaw Hastings, which Dahl would have seen every day as he worked, and out of sight behind him, is a large contact sheet of fifty-six photos of Olivia smiling happily. Even the tartan rug which he used on cold days has Olivia's nametape stuck inside it.

'When I am up here I see only the paper I am writing on, and my mind is far away with Willy Wonka or James or Mr Fox or Danny or whatever else I am trying to cook up,' wrote Dahl. 'The room itself is of no consequence. It is out of focus, a place for dreaming and floating and whistling in the wind, as soft and silent and murky as a womb.'

The accumulated objects of a lifetime surrounded Dahl in his 'nest'.

Charles Dickens
The joy of designing your own writing room

Writing chalet, Gad's Hill, Higham, Kent; various homes in London

The works and letters of Charles Dickens (1812–70) indicate his obsession with the idea of home, and wherever he wrote, he was most particular about his surroundings. Whenever he was on tour abroad, he always packed his portable rosewood writing desk inlaid with mother-of-pearl, a little piece of home away from home. Back in England, he indulged his keen interest in interior décor in the design of his various writing rooms and studies – at his Gad's Hill home in Kent, and at his London houses at Tavistock House and in Doughty Street, which is now the Charles Dickens Museum. Here, the desk at which he wrote *Great Expectations* and worked on *The Mystery of Edwin Drood* is on permanent display.

Dickens took a close personal interest in all aspects of designing and decorating his homes, including his work spaces to get them exactly how he wanted them, sometimes with unusual results. So when the family's pet raven Grip died, Dickens hired a taxidermist to stuff and mount him in an impressive case, hanging him above his writing desk. (Grip is now on display in the rare book section at the Free Library in Philadelphia.) He also had rows of dummy bookcases with fake book spines installed at Tavistock House and Gad's Hill by his favoured bookbinder Thomas Eeles. These had mainly humorous titles – *Five Minutes in China* (three volumes), *Cats' Lives* (nine volumes) – though some were more personal ('Mag's Diversions' was an early working title for *David Copperfield*).

His most intriguing working space was his writing chalet at Gad's Hill. This was a prefabricated two-storey Swiss chalet

> *His most intriguing working space was his writing chalet at Gad's Hill. This was a prefabricated two-storey Swiss chalet given to him by the French actor Charles Fechter.*

The study at Gad's Hill Place, now a school.

given to him as a Christmas present by the French actor Charles Fechter. It came in nearly a hundred pieces in fifty-eight packing cases via the local train station. Dickens, who enjoyed a session of DIY, was very excited by this prospect of his own writing cabin and initially tried to put it together himself with some friends, but in the end admitted defeat (partly perhaps because the instructions were all in French). He then called in the stage carpenter of the Lyceum Theatre in London to finish it.

Unlike most writing huts, it was not in his back garden but on land he owned across the road from his house. The chalet was oriented to allow views of the River Thames in the distance, and he set up a telescope so that he could watch passing boats. To reach it, he designed and built a kind of underpass tunnel to avoid dealing with the road traffic and mud. Dickens worked in the top-floor study of the chalet, including on *A Tale of Two Cities* and *Our Mutual Friend*, from 1865 until the day of his death in 1870. This room also contained numerous mirrors installed at Dickens' behest, partly to increase the light but also probably to help him observe himself as he rehearsed for his public readings.

In his 1872 biography of Dickens, John Forster quotes the novelist's son-in-law Charles Collins' description of the objects Dickens kept on the desk: 'There was a French bronze group representing a duel with swords, fought by a couple of very fat toads ... a statuette of a dog-fancier ... the long gilt leaf with the rabbit sitting erect upon its haunches, the huge paper-knife often held in his hand during his public readings, and the little fresh green cup ornamented with leaves and blossoms of the cowslip, in which a few fresh flowers were always placed every morning.'

Wherever he worked, Dickens used a goose quill pen to write, from 9 a.m. until 2 p.m. (when he then went for a long walk), and on one side of the paper only (except for letters). Initially he preferred black ink, but from 1843 he moved to blue paper and blue ink, which dried more quickly.

The writing chalet, now sadly in need of complete restoration.

Emily Dickinson
Embracing the solitude

Bedroom, Amherst, Massachusetts

Poet Emily Dickinson's (1830–86) bedroom became central to her life as she increasingly withdrew from her family's busy social whirl. When her niece Martha came to visit her in her bedroom, Emily pretended to lock the door with an invisible key and said: 'Matty, here's freedom.'

The key element in Dickinson's writing routine was solitude. She wrote virtually her entire life's work of around 1,800 poems in her bedroom at the family home in Amherst, Massachusetts. Known as the Homestead, this is where she was born in 1830 and is now a museum dedicated to her memory.

Her airy 15ft (4.5m) square by 10ft (3m) high room has the best light and views in the house and also enabled Emily to hear people talking in the street below. On the walls hung pictures of her favourite writers – Thomas Carlyle, Elizabeth Barrett Browning and George Eliot.

Following a major renovation of her bedroom between 2013 and 2015, it is now historically accurate, including reproduction pink-flowered wallpaper. The nineteenth-century floorboards were uncovered, complete with worn areas where Emily put her feet when she got out of bed in the mornings and a trail from her writing stand to her bedside bureau.

Although the small, dark wood bed in the room is Emily's, the tiny writing stand (described by Martha as '18-inches square, with a drawer deep enough to take in her ink bottle, paper and pen') and the chest of drawers (where the bulk of her poems were discovered) are careful reproductions, as the originals, including her writing chair, are part of the Emily Dickinson archive at Harvard University.

You can now experience what it was like to work in Emily's bedroom as the museum offers two-hour slots in which you can be alone in the room to write.

Dickinson found freedom to write at the tiny desk in her bedroom.

Arthur Conan Doyle
The portable writing 'room'

Portable desk; study, South Norwood, London

Not all writing desks are substantial pieces of furniture. The writing box – with a sloping top and space inside for ink and paper – has been popular since the eighteenth century. Dr Samuel Johnson remarked of the poet Alexander Pope that: 'It was punctually required that his writing-box should be set upon his bed before he rose'; and playwright Oliver Goldsmith, Lord Byron, Jane Austen and the Brontë sisters were all similarly attached to their writing boxes. A laptop contraption was, however, not sufficient for the creator of Sherlock Holmes.

Sir Arthur Ignatius Conan Doyle (1859–1930) liked to write on the move so much that in 1925 he commissioned Parisian luxury luggage-maker Goyard to make him a very special writing trunk. Closed, it looks like an attractive travel trunk of normal size and weight. Opened wide, however, it transforms into a writing desk, with a bookcase, typewriter and storage space. Conan Doyle was delighted with the trunk, as by this time he was making regular lecturing trips around the world on which he talked about his famous fictional detective as well as his passion for spiritualism. Goyard was pleased with the result, too, and produced six more. Conan Doyle's trunk was put up for sale by antique collector and gallery owner Timothy Oulton in 2019, priced at £96,000.

When not on his travels, Conan Doyle wrote in the study at his home in South Norwood, London, using a Parker Duofold fountain pen for his later Sherlock Holmes stories. 'As to my hours of work, when I am keen on a book I am prepared to work all day,

> 'As to my hours of work, when I am keen on a book I am prepared to work all day, with an hour or two of walk or siesta in the afternoon.'

Conan Doyle's groundbreaking mobile office.

with an hour or two of walk or siesta in the afternoon,' he wrote in an article for *The Strand* magazine in December 1924. Writer and founder of *The Idler* magazine Robert Barr described the study and its unusual contents in an interview with Conan Doyle for *McClure's Magazine* in November 1894.

> The workbench stands in the corner – one of those flat-topped desks so prevalent in England. The English author does not seem to take kindly to the haughty, roller-top American desk, covered with transparent varnish and twenty-three patents. There is a bookcase, filled with solid historical volumes for the most part. The most remarkable feature of the room is a series of water-color drawings done by Conan Doyle's father. The drawings by Mr. Doyle's father are most weird and imaginative, being in art something like what Edgar Allan Poe's stories are in fiction. There are harpoons on the wall, for Doyle has been a whale fisher in his time, and has the skull of a polar bear and the stuffed body of an Iceland falcon to show that his aim was accurate.

One of Conan Doyle's first writing desks can be seen at his old school Stonyhurst College in Lancashire. Among the treasures in the school's museum is the writer's old school desk, into which he carved his name.

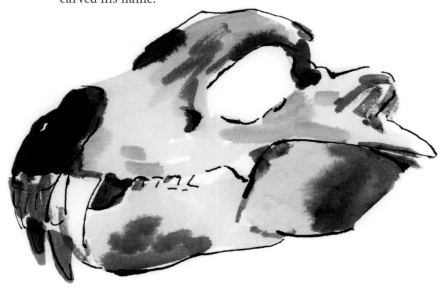

£96,000

Ian Fleming
The stiff routine of a working holiday

Study, Oracabessa Bay, Jamaica

Fleming's Jamaican
writing room came with
a view that he found too
distracting.

In his book *On Writing: A Memoir of the Craft*, novelist Stephen King says there is no fairy-tale writer's muse who magically descends. 'You have to do all the grunt labor,' he emphasizes. And the spot that Ian Fleming (1908–64), creator of James Bond, chose to do his grunting was Jamaica.

More precisely it was his holiday bungalow Goldeneye in Oracabessa Bay (also home to playwright and composer Noël Coward's Firefly Estate home) that stimulated Fleming. He bought the property, complete with private beach and reef, in 1946. From 1952 onwards Fleming travelled to Goldeneye and from January to March worked on a new Bond adventure over an intensive two-month period. Fleming admitted that he doubted the books would have been written if he had not been living in what he describe as 'the gorgeous vacuum of a Jamaican holiday'.

When Fleming bought Goldeneye, it was a simple building, unfussily furnished (Coward described it as looking like a medical clinic) and Fleming worked at an appropriately simple corner desk on a wooden chair with a circular spoked back. Nearby, he kept reference books about the region's flora and fauna, including *The Field Guide to Birds of the West Indies* by an ornithologist with the inspiring name of James Bond. Each morning he would wake up at about 7.30 a.m. and go for a swim (without trunks) before breakfasting in the garden, usually on his favourite scrambled eggs and Blue Mountain coffee. At around 9 a.m., he then went inside to his study, closed the glass-less jalousie windows to ensure he had a cool place to work without the distractions of a beautifully sunny view and settled down to writing.

Fleming worked on an Imperial typewriter – he said he found typing with six fingers less exhausting than writing by hand – producing 2,000 words every day by around noon. At this

Typewriters

The development of the typewriter in the late nineteenth century – what Mark Twain called the 'new-fangled writing machine' – had a profound effect on writers' working lives. Twain was the first to send in a typescript manuscript to a publisher on one: his memoir *Life on the Mississippi* (though it was actually typed by his secretary, Isabel Lyon). Initially he adored his Remington model's speed, ease of use and lack of ink blots, but eventually fell out of love with it because it was 'full of caprices, full of defects – devilish ones'. It was also a major investment, costing a whopping $125 in 1871.

However, many twentieth-century writers developed a strong bond with their typewriters. Screenwriter Larry McMurtry even thanked his Hermes 3000 in his speech after winning a Golden Globe for *Brokeback Mountain* in 2006. It is, he said: 'surely one of the noblest instruments of European genius.' And when Danielle Steel (see page 148) discovered in 2015 that the typing paper she'd used since she was a teenager had been discontinued she tweeted mournfully: 'Losing an old friend ... my old typewriter and I are very sad!'

This intimate connection with the typewriter is one of its strongest appeals to writers. Henry James found the loud clack of its keys inspirational and Anthony Burgess revelled in the very physicality of typing (pointing out too that the sounds of typing indicated you were actually working, rather than just daydreaming). Both he and Will Self have also argued that typewriters actually improve your work by making you think carefully before committing to the page. 'The typewriter makes for lucidity, but I am not sure that it encourages subtlety,' agreed T.S. Eliot, owner of a Smith Corona. And of course, they look rather stylish too. Travel writer Jan Morris wrote on the brilliant red Olivetti Valentine designed by Ettore Sottsass and Perry King.

They can also be surprisingly valuable. Cormac McCarthy wrote *The Road*, *No Country for Old Men* and *All the Pretty Horses* on his light blue Lettera 32 Olivetti, bought in 1963 for $50. He estimated that he produced some five million words on it. When Christie's auctioned it for charity in 2009, it went for $254,500. McCarthy loyally replaced it with another Olivetti, one that cost only $11.

point, he headed off for lunch and a siesta, before returning at
5 p.m. to 6 p.m. to continue his morning's work, with essentially
no editing. Finished pages were then stored safely away in the
bottom left-hand drawer of the desk. This rapid and disciplined
approach of which he was proud was then repeated every day
until by the end of his stay he had another finished novel. After
finishing his first Bond novel, *Casino Royale* (which actually
only took a month), he treated himself to a rather glamorous
replacement, a Royal Quiet Deluxe Portable gold-plated
typewriter from the Royal Typewriter Company in New York, on
which he revised *Casino Royale* and wrote subsequent adventures.
It cost $174. He typed double-spaced on folio-size paper, slightly
larger than A4, chain-smoking as he worked on custom-made
cigarettes from Morland's of Grosvenor Square back in London.

For those writers unable to afford a similar hideaway,
Fleming advised in an article 'How to Write a Thriller' in the May
1963 issue of the now defunct *Books and Bookmen* magazine that:
'I can recommend hotel bedrooms as far removed from
your usual "life" as possible. Your anonymity in these drab
surroundings and your lack of friends and distractions in the
strange locale will create a vacuum
which should force you into a writing
mood and, if your pocket is
shallow, into a mood which will
also make you write fast and
with application.'

Thomas Hardy
A bedroom with a view

Bedroom, Higher Bockhampton, Dorset

Sometimes the most important thing about a writer's room is not the space itself but what it looks out on. Few writers are as intimately associated with their local surroundings as Thomas Hardy (1840–1928). His novels and poems reflect his lifelong love of nature, the Wessex countryside a direct mirror of his personal experience and an ever-present character in his works. The notebooks that he kept as an inspiration to his work are filled with the literary equivalents of painters' sketches, notes about weather, sunsets and the sounds of nature.

Hardy was born and grew up in a cottage in Higher Bockhampton, near Dorchester in Dorset. The cottage is at the northern edge of the mixed woodland and heath of Thorncombe Wood, which gives on to Black Heath, inspirations for the fictional Egdon Heath in Hardy's *The Return of the Native* and *The Mayor of Casterbridge*. Hardy lived at this cob-and-thatch cottage until he was thirty-four. It was here, in his bedroom, that he wrote *Far from the Madding Crowd* and *Under the Greenwood Tree*, which first introduces his Wessex landscape.

Hardy's bedroom was a sparse affair, initially shared with his much younger brother Henry. He wrote at a window seat and small wooden desk, from which he could gaze out through the window on to the surrounding countryside. The first stanza of his poem 'Domicilium', completed when he was sixteen, describes the cottage, and shows that even from this early age he was determined to make nature central to his work. The cottage reappears in *Under the Greenwood Tree* as the lightly fictionalized home of the tranter, or carrier: 'a long, low cottage with a hipped roof of thatch, having dormer windows breaking up into the eaves, a chimney standing in the middle of the ridge and another at each end.' One of those dormers was the window of Hardy's bedroom where he wrote the book.

Hardy wrote of his cottage: 'It faces west, and round the back and sides/High beeches, bending, hang a veil of boughs.'

Ernest Hemingway
A bedroom to stand in

Bedroom, Havana, Cuba

Although some critics suggest that the rise in the use of standing desks over the last decade is some kind of health fad, the truth is that many writers have preferred to work vertically. Among the keenest standers was Ernest Hemingway (1899–1961), for whom it was a habit formed even before the injuries he sustained in two plane crashes in 1954 made it painful for him to sit for long periods.

As a birthday present, Hemingway's wife Mary built him a four-storey tower at his Finca Vigía home in Cuba, but he much preferred to write in his bedroom, closer to the hustle and bustle of the house. Here he worked on top of a bookcase placed next to a wall, his typewriter at chest height in the middle, flanked by stacks of books and papers. Nearby was his word-count chart, as Hemingway was very conscientious about hitting his 500-ish words a day mark, though he upped his game for *The Sun Also Rises* to nearer 2,000.

The room was decorated in typical Hemingway fashion, with a stuffed gazelle head on the wall marking one of his successful hunts, and a leopard skin on the top of his wardrobe.

The room was decorated in typical Hemingway fashion, with a stuffed gazelle head on the wall marking one of his successful hunts, and a leopard skin on the top of his wardrobe. There were, naturally, various full bookshelves, on which he kept odds and ends, including a giraffe made of wood beads, a monkey holding cymbals and a tin model of a US Navy biplane. He did have a desk too, but as his biographer Aaron Hotchner notes in *Papa Hemingway: A Personal Memoir*, he never used it. Here's Hotchner's list of what Hemingway kept on it:

Hemingway's bedroom featured trophies from his big game hunting days.

- stacks of letters grouped together using rubber bands, bullfighting magazines and clippings from old newspapers
- a small sack of carnivores' teeth
- two clocks (unwound)
- shoehorns
- an unfilled pen in an onyx holder
- a zebra, warthog, rhino and lion, each carved out of wood and in a row
- a stuffed toy lion
- miscellaneous souvenirs of his travels
- shotgun shells

He worked here from early in the morning, usually from first light (around 6.30 a.m.), sometimes with his pets around, including Black Dog his spring spaniel. 'There is no one to disturb you,' he said, 'and it is cool or cold and you come to your work and warm as you write.' He always wore loafers and stood on a rug made out of an antelope skin. He knocked off about noon when he felt 'empty' but with an idea of what would come next tomorrow when he started writing again – he said that wait until the next day's writing began was hard to get through. At this point he would go for a walk or a swim in his pool. He might also have a drink, since despite his reputation for knocking back alcohol, he never drank while writing. Nor did he usually write on Sundays, believing it to be bad luck.

He would start with a pencil, writing on thin onionskin paper on a reading board on top of the bookcase-desk, admitting that 'wearing down seven number-two pencils is a good day's work'. When he was well underway, especially when it came to dialogue, he would switch to his typewriter – he had various during his lifetime, including several Coronas, an Underwood Noiseless Portable and a Royal Quiet Deluxe (see Ian Fleming, page 68). Among the books he wrote at Finca Vigía were *For Whom the Bell Tolls*, *A Moveable Feast* and *The Old Man and the Sea*.

Victor Hugo
A view towards France

Rooftop writing room, St Peter Port, Guernsey

Victor Hugo (1802–85) arrived in Guernsey in 1855, having gone into exile from his native France after crossing political swords with Napoleon III. He lost no time in buying Hauteville House, a large white villa at 38 Rue Hauteville, St Peter Port, and renovating it to his exact specifications. Most of the rooms were done out in a kind of opulent Gothic style, but in 1861 he added his own writing room to the top floor, known as the Lookout, where he wrote his masterpieces *Les Misérables* and *Toilers of the Sea*.

The Lookout has the feel of a conservatory or greenhouse perched on the top of the house rather than in the back garden, with large glass windows on three sides and a glass roof. Hugo added mirrors to accentuate the feeling of light and so the sea could be seen on all walls. Measuring nearly 20ft by 10ft (6m by 3m), it was inspired by the Crystal Palace in London built to house the Great Exhibition of 1851 – he called it his 'Crystal Room'. Hugo started writing in it in 1862 before it was completely finished.

Over the next fifteen years of his exile, he wrote at his standing desk by a sea-facing window, enjoying panoramic views over the town and the islands of Herm and Sark, as well as (on a clear day) to France. In one poem he described being deep in thought as he writes at his window, watching the seagulls, the ships and the tide coming in and out.

In a letter to his friend the French journalist Auguste Vacquerie, Hugo wrote that 'the sky and the sea add flavour' to the room. 'Any spot is good for daydreaming so long as it is in an obscure corner and the horizon is vast.'

Here, as in the rest of the house, he used blue and white ceramic Delft tiles to decorate the walls. It was comfortably though not luxuriously furnished, with a three-tiered sofa on which he left his finished pages to dry. A circle of glass on the floor allowed light through to the floor below.

Hugo's Lookout: roasting hot in the summer, freezing cold in the winter.

There was also a Louis XV stove in the room but that did not help much with the heating. At the inauguration of a statue to Hugo in Candie Gardens, his son Georges said: 'It is so hot in the Lookout in the summer that the paint peels and the mercury of the mirrors melts like fire ... If the summer heat was savage under these panes, the cold in winter was freezing. Without overcoat, bareheaded, always so calm and serene, he still wrote. The wind blew in through the wide open windows like a hurricane.'

Hugo spent his mornings writing here. 'A writer who gets up before daybreak and finishes his day at noon has done well,' he wrote. He told French journalist Paul Stapfer, who visited him at Hautville, that he had two raw eggs and a cup of cold coffee for breakfast

'At 11 a.m., covered in perspiration because of the fire of his work and the stove that heated his greenhouse in winter, he stripped naked and, in the English style, mopped himself with cold water.'

before setting down to write. This did not always go well, perhaps not least because, as Stapfer remarked, 'disorder and chaos had their empire in this upper room'.

Stapfer added a strange anecdote to his account of Hugo's writing routine.

At 11 a.m., covered in perspiration because of the fire of his work and the stove that heated his greenhouse in winter, he stripped naked and, in the English style, mopped himself with cold water which had been out all night in the air. People who were passing along Hauteville Street at this time who raised their eyes to his glass cage would have seen a white apparition. Energetic friction with horsehair gloves was the second and indispensable part of this carefully tuned routine.

In the afternoons, he would go for walks around the island and visit his lover, Juliette Drouet.

'So long as you write
what you wish to write,
that is all that matters;
and whether it matters
for ages or only for
hours, nobody can say.'

Virginia Woolf

'I must keep to my own style and go on in my own way; and though I may never succeed again in that, I am convinced that I should totally fail in any other.'

Jane Austen

Samuel Johnson
The stimulation of a view from the top

Garret, London

Perhaps the greatest cliché about writers' rooms is the image of
an intense and penniless young man or woman, scribbling away
furiously in a tiny garret. The most famous of garret-workers
was Dr Samuel Johnson (1709–84), who in the late 1740s rented
the top room of the townhouse at No. 17 Gough Street in London
(the Dr Johnson Museum since 1913), where he wrote his famous
dictionary, published in 1755.

Like all garrets, being at the top of the house meant that
it was very simply furnished and was the only room in the
house without pannelling, having simple plaster walls and no
decorative mouldings. It was reached via a winding staircase
which led onto a low-ceilinged room covering the whole of
the top floor, an open space without any dividers. This layout
has remained largely unchanged. The room today is used for
exhibitions, talks and workshops, but it was in here that Johnson
commanded a team of half a dozen amanuenses to produce his
Dictionary of the English Language.

'He had an upper room fitted up like a counting house for
the purpose,' wrote Johnson's equally famous biographer James
Boswell, 'in which he gave the copyists their several tasks.' These
assistants worked at tall desks, sets of bookshelves set against the
wall. Johnson himself was a bad sleeper, partly due to the range of
illnesses from which he suffered, so he tended to rise late in the
morning to begin work.

Johnson wrote several pieces about the garret in the magazine
he published, *The Rambler*. In his lighthearted 1751 article 'The
Advantages of Living in a Garret', he argued that the garret's
popularity as a space in which to write was not due to its cheap
price, its remoteness from visitors ('who talk incessantly of
beer, or linen, or a coat'), its relative quiet or its inspiring views.
Instead, he pointed out 'that the professors of literature generally

Johnson was under
no illusion that writing
in a garret guaranteed
literary success.

reside in the highest stories has been immemorially observed', mentioning, for example, that the Muses lived at the top of Mount Olympus. From this high vantage point, Johnson wrote of 'the pleasure with which a wise man looks down upon the confused and erratick state of the world moving below him'.

He acknowledged, however, that it could not work miracles. 'That a garret will make every man a wit,' he admitted, 'I am very far from supposing; I know there are some who would continue blockheads even on the summit of the Andes, or on the peak of Teneriffe.'

Once the dictionary was published, Johnson kept the garrett on, but turned it into a private study rather than a co-working space, the one room in the house where his beloved wife never entered. One visitor was the then celebrated music scholar Dr Charles Burney, father of the novelist Fanny Burney, who wrote this account of his visit: 'After dinner, Mr Johnson proposed

'That a garret will make every man a wit, I am very far from supposing; I know there are some who would continue blockheads even on the summit of the Andes, or on the peak of Teneriffe.'

to Mr Bernie to go up with him into his Garret, in which, being accepted, he found about five or six Greek folios, a deal writing desk, and a chair and a half. Johnson, giving to his guest the entire seat, totted himself on one with only three legs and one arm.' Boswell also seems to have liked it. 'The place seemed to be very favourable for retirement and meditation,' he wrote. 'Johnson told me, that he went up thither without mentioning it to his servant, when he wanted to study, secure from interruption.' A later visitor was the writer and philosopher Thomas Carlyle, who made his way up the steps in 1832 and described the garret as a 'hayloft'.

Judith Kerr
The stimulus of pets and loved ones

Attic, London

The writer and illustrator Judith Kerr (1923–2019) worked for more than fifty years in the same three-storey, terraced Victorian house in Barnes, London, in the attic studio office up two flights of stairs. She continued to navigate these into her nineties. Her home, family and pets were constant inspirations to her, providing the models (and names) for the family in her series of Mog books, while the kitchen cupboards in *The Tiger Who Came to Tea* were replicas of those in her own kitchen.

It had two benefits. Firstly, it was not easy for people to come and disturb her while she was working. But equally importantly, her working room was right next to her husband Nigel Kneale's, the science fiction writer behind the Quatermass serials on television. Whenever stuck on something, they would visit each other for support, and break for lunch at the same time. After he died, Kerr left his typewriter on the desk in his study, unmoved.

Kerr's room was painted white with white furniture and windows providing plenty of light. It included a large bookcase full of art books, a straw hat given to her by her son and a poster advertising a reading of her and her writer father's books by German actor Martin Held. She used the same drawing board throughout her working life, a desk with Formica fixed to the top bought for £5 in her twenties and carefully preserved ever since. Around her were plenty of soft pencils, dozens of crayons (sorted in jars according to colour) and her Winsor & Newton inks. There was also a small mirror on her desk to help with drawing her characters' hands. She once described the feeling of going up to this room as 'awfully like coming home'.

Kerr had a series of cats. The original Mog used to sit on her lap as she worked and fiddled with Kerr's brush, while her final cat Katinka developed a habit of sitting in Kerr's working chair when she got up.

Kerr said walking into her writing room always felt like coming home.

Stephen King
Getting the desk size right

Attic, Bangor, Maine

Writing routines are not set in stone. They can – and should – be adjusted if they are not working. Canadian novelist Stephen King (1947–) – best known for *Carrie*, *Pet Sematary* and *The Shining* – has made major changes to his desk, his music habits and even his writing implements.

King aims to write about six pages or 2,000 words a day over three or four hours, starting work around 8 a.m. every morning with a cup of tea and then finishing for the day usually around 1.30 p.m. (unless he has been writing particularly fast). Although he now writes on laptops and has used Olivetti and Underwood typewriters in the past, King still sometimes writes in longhand. On the plus side, he says it gives him time to think and polish at the first draft stage; on the down side, it's much slower. Once his writing session is over, the rest of the day is spent with family, reading or other domestic business.

His routine is very regulated, sitting in the same seat and keeping his paperwork in the same place, which he says helps to concentrate his mind on the task in hand. He is very keen on the idea of writers having a definite goal for each writing session, whatever the wordcount. He argues that it's important to have a room to work which has as few distractions as possible and a door to close to keep people from coming in, a statement that you are 'at work' in your sanctuary and should not be disturbed. King is aiming for conditions conducive to what he describes as 'creative sleep', with the repetitive element as a kind of rite which prepares you for the ceremony of writing in the same way that your routine of going to bed helps you get ready for sleep.

King attributes a key part of his success to his choice of desks. As an aspiring young writer he was very keen to get an enormous desk, the very opposite of the dropdown half-moon shelf desk on which Lousia May Alcott wrote *Little Women* in her bedroom.

King found a smaller desk much easier to work on.

He did indeed buy a huge desk for his home in 1981, once he had become a successful established author, but found that for the following few years it did not help him write at all (though he was also going through a chaotic period of substance abuse too, which cannot have helped).

Once he quit alcohol and drugs, he threw the desk out and made his writing room much more homely. He started by putting a new – much smaller and handmade – desk in a fairly inconspicuous corner of the room, away from the window and under an eave, rather than making it the centrepiece. Then he added rugs, a sofa and a television, and made it inviting

His routine is very regulated, sitting in the same seat and keeping his paperwork in the same place, which he says helps to concentrate his mind on the task in hand.

for his children, whom he encouraged to come up and watch sport or films with him. As he says in his book about the art of writing: 'Life isn't a support system for art. It's the other way around.'

Another thing that has changed is his attitude to music. As a young writer he listened to music while he wrote, partly to encourage him to keep the pace of the action up, but he now generally only does so towards the end of a writing session while he is going over that morning's work.

Rudyard Kipling
The right kind of ink

Study, Dummerston, Vermont; study, Burwash, East Sussex

The creator of *Kim*, Mowgli and 'The Man Who Would Be King', Rudyard Kipling (1892–1936) had a very conservative taste in writing rooms. At Naulakha, the American home he had built for himself in Vermont, he was surrounded by packed bookshelves, a sturdy desk (on which he scratched 'Oft was I weary as I toiled at thee', a slight misquote from Henry Wadsworth Longfellow), a solid chair and a brick fireplace with 'The night cometh when no man can work' from St John's Gospel carved into it. Although he was a gregarious man, his wife Carrie arranged it so that her office – which became known as the 'dragon's chamber' – was adjacent to his and so he was able to prevent any unwanted visitors.

Kipling's panelled study at his home at Bateman's in East Sussex where he wrote the 'Just So' stories was similarly straightforward. He worked in the mornings, finding inspiration by walking back and forth on his Indian rugs. The chair legs were slightly too long for Kipling, so he had them raised on blocks so he could comfortably reach the seventeenth-century walnut desk by the window. In his autobiography *Something of Myself*, he listed the items he kept on his 10ft (3m) long desk:

- a lacquer, canoe-shaped pen-tray full of old pens and brushes
- a wooden box for paperclips and rubber bands
- a tin box containing pins
- another box of miscellaneous items including emery paper and small screwdrivers
- a paper-weight, probably owned by Warren Hastings who led the formation of the British rule in India
- a long ruler
- a penwiper to clean pens

Kipling preferred to write using the blackest possible ink.

Next to his desk he had two large globes.

In the afternoons, he took a walk in the surrounding countryside as an aid to inspiration before returning to read on his day bed in the study and smoke away. This was part of his personal 'drift, wait, obey' approach to writing and 'hatching' his ideas – to try not to think consciously about what he was writing all the time, but allow what he called his 'Daemon', or writing muse, time to consider things. Here again, Carrie kept a watchful eye on comings and goings, or as the writer P.G. Wodehouse described it, 'rigidly excluded [him] from the world'.

What was most important to Kipling was his ink, as he was not keen on his typewriter ('The beastly thing simply won't spell,' he complained). Kipling recounts how he demanded the blackest possible ink. He said blue-blacks were an abomination to his Daemon. Additionally, he was not a fan of everyday bottled ink. Ideally, he said, 'I would have kept an ink boy to grind me Indian ink.' This mixture of glue, bones, tar, soot and pitch came in solid stick form, which needed to be pounded then mixed with water using a brush to make a useable liquid.

Indeed much of his working routine centred on his writing materials. While he was in India, he was very fond of his hand-dipped Waverley nib ink pen, which he used with an octagonal penholder made out of agate. When this broke, he experimented with a series of others with less happy results – he called fountain pens 'geyser-pens' and said that he 'tried pump-pens with glass insides, but they were of "intolerable entrails"'. A housemaid kept the desk tidy and clean, making sure there was always an adequate supply of paper and ink every day.

Kipling was not the tidiest of writers, and contemporaries report that he used to dip his pens deeply, and jerkily, into his inkpot and get ink everywhere. He was described by one friend as spotted with ink 'like a Dalmatian dog', especially during hot weather when he dressed all in white.

Ink

Ink has been the reliable companion to writers for centuries, but one key issue is what colour to use. George Eliot, the author of *Middlemarch*, was particularly scathing in her 1856 essay 'Silly Novels by Lady Novelists' when she wrote: 'It is clear that they write in elegant boudoirs, with violet-colored ink and a ruby pen.'

Green is rather frowned upon (though the head of MI6 traditionally signs letters in this colour), but rather than pick one, several writers simply vary it. Quentin Tarantino writes his screenplays using red and black felt tips, and novelist Amos Oz used blue for fiction and black for non-fiction.

Author Neil Gaiman, who usually writes his first drafts with a fountain pen, uses at least two pens, each with different coloured inks, including brown. At the end of a day's writing, the colours provide him with a quick and easy way of determining how much work he has done.

American writer William Faulkner even wanted to print his 1929 novel *The Sound and the Fury* in different coloured inks to help the reader cope with the complex jumps in time, but the right technology was not then in place. Here is Isaac Newton's advice 'To make excellent Ink':

½ lb of Galls cut in pieces or grosly beaten, ¼ lb of Gumm Arabick cut or broken. Put 'em into a Quart of strong beer or Ale. Let 'em stand a month stopt up, stirring them now & then. At ye end of the moneth put in 1 or 1 ½ of copperas (Too much copperas makes ye ink apt to turn yellow.) Stir it & use it. Stop it up for some time with a paper prickt full of holes & let it stand in ye sunn. When you take out ink put in so much strong beer & it will endure many years. Water makes it apt to mold. Wine does not. The air also if it stand open inclines it to mold.

D.H. Lawrence
Four walls do not a writing room make

Various trees, Taos County, New Mexico

The talisman of a desk or a favourite view from a window is not for every writer. D.H. Lawrence (1885–1930) found particular comfort and inspiration from writing close to or under (and indeed about) trees around the world, though the stories of him allegedly climbing mulberry trees naked are probably fanciful.

He particularly enjoyed the trees at the Kiowa Ranch, now known as the D.H. Lawrence Ranch, in Taos County, New Mexico. Here, living in simple cabins amid 160 acres of rural calm, 8,500ft (2,600m) high near Lobo Mountain, Lawrence wrote *The Plumed Serpent* (1926), *St Mawr* (1925) and *The Woman Who Rode Away* (1924), accompanied by his wife Frieda and various friends, most notably the painter and socialite Dorothy Brett. Just outside his door was a large ponderosa pine that Lawrence described as a 'guardian angel' and under which he wrote during the morning on a simple bench.

Just outside his door was a large ponderosa pine that Lawrence described as a 'guardian angel' and under which he wrote during the morning on a simple bench.

In 1929 it was immortalized by Georgia O'Keeffe in a painting, *The Lawrence Tree*, after she spent several weeks at the ranch, working at the same bench.

Brett wrote about her time at the ranch in her book *Lawrence and Brett: A Friendship* (1933), describing his tree-based working routine. 'In the quiet, still morning, with your copy-book under your arm and your fountain pen, you go off away into the woods. Sometimes one can glimpse you through the trees, sitting leaning up against the trunk of a pine tree, in your blue shirt, white corduroy pants, and big, pointed straw hat.' She also recalled looking for him to call in to lunch and discovering him 'leaning

'I go off by myself into the woods and write each morning,' said Lawrence.

against a tree, in a deep dream, abstracted, in the world of the story you are writing'.

Lawrence also enjoyed writing among the trees close to where he lived in the Black Forest village of Ebersteinburg, Baden-Baden, Germany. 'I go off by myself into the woods and write each morning,' he wrote in a letter to the painter Jan Juta in June, 1921. 'I find a forest such a strange stimulus – the trees are like living company. They seem to give off something dynamic and secret, and anti-human – or non-human. Especially fir-trees.'

During these outdoor writing sessions, he produced his 1922 novel *Aaron's Rod* as well as other work. 'One of the few places that my soul will haunt, when I am dead, will be this. [...] I can't leave these trees. They have taken some of my soul.' Indeed, he worked them into the text of the novel, describing how they moved in the wind and seemed to converse with each other.

His best-known work was *Lady Chatterley's Lover*, written under a large umbrella pine in a wood near the Villa Mirenda (also known as Villa L'Arcipresso), Scandicci, near Florence, Italy. In her foreword to *The First Lady Chatterley* (Lawrence wrote two later versions beforethe famous final title), Frieda explained:

> He had to walk a little way by the olive trees to get to his umbrella pine. Thyme and mint tufts grew along the path and purple anemones and wild gladioli and carpets of violets and myrtle shrubs. White, calm oxen were plowing. There he would sit, almost motionless except for his swift writing. He would be so still that the lizards would run over him and the birds hop close around him.

He wrote most of the morning and after a break for lunch, read the new work to Frieda.

Astrid Lindgren
A personal writing language

Study, Stockholm

A bronze statue of Lindgren in her home town of Vimmerby depicts her seated in this room with her typewriter. Visitors can sit on a spare seat opposite her.

Astrid Lindgren (1907–2002) wrote many children's books and is one of the world's most translated writers, her international fame resting particularly on her Pippi Longstocking series.

The flat in Stockholm where she lived from 1941 until her death is now open to the public. Particularly inviting is her book-lined study, the walls covered in pictures and with a lovely view through the window to the Vasaparken park above her simple desk. It's a home rather than a full-blown museum, largely untouched since her death.

Lindgren's writing routine was similarly straightforward. She worked on her books in the mornings, preferring to write in her small bed. She wrote in pencil in notepads, typing up each chapter as it was finished on her Facit Privat typewriter, on view on the desk in the study. She wrote fast, commenting that she felt the book had already been finished by the time she started writing and that she had only to type it out. After a light lunch, she headed for work in the afternoon at the Rabén & Sjögren publishing house where she was a children's book editor.

Less straightforward was how she wrote her books. Before Pippi Longstocking brought her fame, she trained as a secretary, and when it came to writing her stories she filled her notebooks with early drafts in shorthand, all in the main Swedish method called Melin, based on the German system Gabelsberger. She was a prolific writer and the vast amount of literary material she left behind in the country's national archive is the largest ever donated by a single person in Sweden, representing around 460ft (140m) of shelving. It is also one of the world's largest collections of shorthand writings, comprising around 670 shorthand notepads. For many years, these notebooks were regarded as undecipherable but now decoding work, aided by digital text recognition techniques, is underway.

Jack London
A life outside the writing room

Porch/study, Glen Ellen, California

London was equally happy working inside on his desk or outside with a board stretched over his legs.

Jack London (1876–1916), the prolific American author best known for his animal-focused novels *The Call of the Wild* and *White Fang*, led a short but exciting life, which included a stint in the Klondike during the Gold Rush, a job as an oyster pirate and sailor, working as a war correspondent and time in prison for vagrancy.

With that history behind him, he happily settled into life in his cottage at his northern California ranch, now the Jack London State Historic Park. In order not to disturb his wife Charmian, he slept in a side porch here, since he often rose early (about 5 a.m.) to write. Between the walls of the porch (which is where he died), he hung a wire – what he described as his 'clothes line' – onto which he attached dozens of notes and ideas on small square pieces of white paper. He stopped for a simple breakfast, then moved to his more comfortable study next to the porch to write until 11 a.m. or noon, and sometimes wrote late at night.

In his early years, when he found it hard to make money from his writing, he rented a typewriter and pawned his coat, suit and bicycle rather than lose them altogether.

The study was a more conventional writing room in which he worked on his 1902 Bar-Lock No. 10 typewriter. This was unusual in several ways – it did not have the standard QWERTY key arrangement, there was no key for exclamation marks and there were separate keyboards for upper- and lower-case letters. In his early years, when he found it hard to make money from his writing, he rented a typewriter and pawned his coat, suit and bicycle rather than lose them altogether.

The room had plenty of natural light from large windows and was lined with bookcases. London was a big reader. 'I regard

books in my library in much the same way that a sea captain regards the charts in his chart-room,' he wrote. 'The student and thinker must have a well-equipped library, and must know his way around that library.' He planned a large personal library to store his collection of 15,000 books at the twenty-six-room dream home named Wolf House that he had built for himself on his ranch. Above it were plans for a 40 by 19ft (12 by 5.8m) writing room. Unfortunately an accidental fire burned the building to the ground just as it was nearing completion in 1913.

He also sometimes wrote outdoors, sitting on a simple chair and balancing his papers on a large board. Indeed, London was a great outdoorsman, spending far more time working on his ranch than on his writing as he grew older, and admitting that he wrote entirely to make money. 'Every time I sit down to write, it is with great disgust,' he said. 'I'd sooner be out in the open, wandering around most any old place.' He was particularly fond of the large 400-year-old oak tree known as Jack's Oak to the side of the

cottage, which he could see from his study's windows. It inspired his play *The Acorn-Planter*.

Alongside his commercial mentality, London always had a strong work ethic. When he started out as a young man, he claimed to write for fifteen hours a day, sometimes forgetting to eat. Like Kurt Vonnegut, he also kept all his early rejection slips, ramming them onto a spike to form a pile that grew to 4ft (1.2m) high. The earliest came from *The Saturday Evening Post*, which said his story 'Sunlanders' was interesting but wondered if he had any other 'tales of a more cheerful nature'. One of his writing techniques was to copy out in longhand many pages of other authors' works, particularly Rudyard Kipling, in an effort to understand the nuts and bolts of their success. By the time he was writing in his cottage, London had a self-imposed daily aim of 1,000 words, which were then edited by Charmian.

Rejection letters

All – *all* – writers are used to rejection from publishers, although it's an urban legend that Herman Melville was turned down with the line: 'First, we must ask, does it have to be a whale?' However T.S. Eliot did suggest to George Orwell that *Animal Farm* was too political for Faber to publish, and offered the plot criticism that 'what was needed (someone might argue), was not more communism but more public-spirited pigs'.

It's certainly true that many rejections have not aged well. 'Stick to your teaching, Miss Alcott,' advised publisher James Fields to the author of *Little Women*. 'You can't write.'

Less harshly, William Golding's *Lord of the Flies* was turned down by Cape who said that: 'It does not seem to us that you have been wholly successful in working out an admittedly promising idea,' and suggested sending it to publisher André Deutsche instead.

But the relationship is not one-way traffic. George Bernard Shaw (see page 142) wrote to a friend in 1895 that: 'I object to publishers. They combine commercial rascality with artistic touchiness and pettiness, without being either good business men or fine judges of literature.'

Hilary Mantel
All the world's a writing room

Writing rooms in Surrey and Budleigh Salterton, Devon

Hilary Mantel (1952–) has a very flexible approach to where she writes, including making notes on public transport or as a passenger in a car (for the very reason that it provides freedom from a desk). Notes are such a central part of her working method that she immediately transcribes her thoughts as soon as she wakes up in the morning. Mantel is certainly not tied to a single space, nor is she picky about writing longhand or on a laptop. Whatever is to hand is fine. 'All the world's a desk' is her motto.

But she still has certain requirements, chiefly silence and, more unusually, a room above ground floor. This includes the top-floor flat of the converted nineteenth-century mental asylum in Surrey where she worked on *Wolf Hall*, and the first-floor flat in Budleigh Salterton where she works today.

At the former, she decorated windows on the three sides of the room in which she worked with gold-coloured curtains, so that when the sun shone she felt like she was in a golden tent. In these surroundings, she wrote on the same gate-legged table she used as a schoolgirl, with decorations including pictures of Thomas Cromwell and Robespierre (a central character in her novel *A Place of Greater Safety*) and bookcases full of books used as research for her novels.

She also set up a useful plotting arrangement in the kitchen. Mantel built up *Wolf Hall* on a mountain of postcards pinned to a large noticeboard, each one representing a scene behind which was pinned scraps of dialogue, detail and other important elements.

For some years, Mantel has worked close to the beach front with an excellent view of the sea. She writes with her desk next to a large window with an ocean outlook. Here, her working routine is to get up early in the morning, write for a while, return to bed, and then after a couple of hours rest, start writing again.

Mantel advises anybody finding problems with a story to simply get away from their desk and do something entirely different, whether it's a walk, a bath or baking a pie.

Margaret Mitchell
Never run out of envelopes

Apartment, Atlanta, Georgia

Margaret Mitchell (1900–49) was a one-novel wonder, but it was a very impressive one. *Gone with the Wind*, her problematic story of Georgia during and after the American Civil War, won her the Pulitzer Prize for fiction, has sold tens of millions of copies and was turned into a genuine Hollywood motion-picture classic.

In 1925, Peggy Marsh, as she preferred to be known, moved with her husband John into the ground-floor Apartment 1 of a brick house at 979 Crescent Avenue, Georgia – now a writer's museum dedicated to her memory – when it was then known as Peachtree Street. It was here that she wrote most of the novel.

The move came hard on the heels of her resigning her post as a reporter at the *Atlanta Journal*, as an old ankle injury began playing up again. Reconciled to convalescing from the comfort of her chair, she continued her childhood habit of extensive reading, relying on John to bring her books from the local library until he suggested she try her hand at actually writing one herself.

She accepted the challenge and began what would be a ten-year writing journey, using childhood memories of stories she had been told about the war as well as heavily researching its history (though there are considerable racist elements to the story, some of which were edited out for the Vivien Leigh and Clark Gable movie). Interestingly, although she read widely, she took very few notes.

Mitchell called the apartment 'The Dump' and it was certainly not as impressive as the mansion she grew up in nearby. Although it could be a bit draughty and was somewhat lacking in natural light, it was not a terrible place in which to work, and she wrote mainly at a plain small wooden folding desk by the window in the living room. There was nothing extraordinary about her technique. 'I had every detail clear in my mind before I sat down to the typewriter [a Remington Portable No. 3],' she said, although

Mitchell's habit of storing her manuscript in various hidden spots all over her home is not recommended.

one oddity was that she wrote the final chapter first and more or less worked backwards to the first.

What was more unusual was what she did with the manuscript in her writing room. As she finished chapters, she put them in manila envelopes so that visitors to the house would not see what she was working on. Gradually these piled up in her living room, and were used to fix the sofa's wobbly leg and as pads for writing down shopping lists and telephone messages. As they grew unwieldly, some were moved to the bedroom where they were stored under the bed, under the floorboards, and in the closet in the hall (which is where she stored many of her books to stop people borrowing them). Occasionally she simply covered them with towels to keep them from prying eyes.

Gradually these piled up in her living room, and were used to fix the sofa's wobbly leg and as pads for writing down shopping lists and telephone messages.

This was how she submitted *Gone with the Wind* when a publisher asked to take a look at her work. He was understandably taken aback at the mountain of manila envelopes, which required him to buy a separate suitcase to transport them.

As if this were not problem enough, none of the chapters or envelopes were numbered and there were several separate drafts of some of the chapters, as well as other slips of paper with additional writing on them. Another issue was that she had forgotten to include the opening chapter. Moreover, some of the chapters were neatly typed on white paper, others were on yellow paper and surrounded by many notes and corrections, including two different death scenarios for Scarlett O'Hara's husband Frank. Even after she had signed a contract for the book, Mitchell was still coming across important chapters/envelopes in her apartment.

Michel de Montaigne
A tower for motivational quotes

Tower, Saint-Michel-de-Montaigne, Dordogne, France

The man who is largely responsible for turning the essay form into a respectable literary genre, French writer, philosopher and politician Michel de Montaigne (1533–92) also understood the need for a dedicated writing room. 'Sorry the man, to my mind,' he wrote, 'who has not in his own home a place to be all by himself, to pay his court privately to himself, to hide.'

Montaigne's place to be all by himself was his large library study on the third floor of a tower next to his chateau in the Dordogne in France. It became his favourite spot after he went into early self-imposed semi-retirement at the ripe old age of thirty-eight in 1571. Some of his work on cold days was done in a side room where there was a fireplace – here, the walls were decorated with various murals, including the *Judgement of Paris*, *Venus and Adonis* and scenes from rural and maritime life. Montaigne added a plaque which describes this as a place to enjoy his freedom, tranquillity and leisure.

In the adjoining larger circular space, he wrote about his thoughts on life, surrounded by various family heirlooms and objects from South America about which he was interested, including wooden swords, jewellery and sticks used in dances. Numerous windows gave him excellent views of his lands outside, and around part of the walls were five rows of curving bookcases. In these he kept his personal library of approximately 1,000 books, while on the ceiling above his head where he worked were dozens of motivational quotes.

Just as writers today often pin encouraging quotes to boards by their desks or attach sticky notes on their monitors, so Montaigne selected some of his favourites from the many classical texts that he read and felt would stimulate him. He then had them painted on virtually all the beams of the ceiling, sometimes replacing older selections with newer maxims as the

Quotes from the Bible and ancient Greek and Roman writers inspired Montaigne in his writing tower.

whim took him. Here, quotes in Greek and Latin from Greek Stoic philosopher Epictetus and odes by Roman poet Horace rub shoulders with various passages from the Bible, especially Ecclesiastes, which he tended to sum up or paraphrase rather than quote exactly. Many of them also pop up in Montaigne's essays, which he usually dictated while standing up or walking around to a secretary sitting at a desk.

Like many motivational quotes, there's something for everybody. Here, for example, is naturalist and naval commander Pliny the Elder writing in the first century AD: *Solum certum nihil esse certi, et homine nihil miserius aut superbius* ('The only certain thing is that nothing is certain, and nothing is more wretched or arrogant than man'). Nearby is a phrase in Greek by philosopher Sextus Empiricus who died around AD 210, which reads simply: 'It is possible and it is not possible.' And here from the Book of Proverbs is: 'Seest thou a man wise in his own conceit? There is more hope of a fool than of him.'

Poet Geoffrey Grigson wrote an atmospheric poem about the writing room and its surroundings in his 1984 collection *Montaigne's Tower and Other Poems*. It describes the tower as being an unmatched place 'for being benign and wise'.

'Work on a good piece of writing proceeds on three levels: a musical one, where it is composed; an architectural one, where it is constructed; and finally, a textile one, where it is woven.'

Walter Benjamin

'Don't write for money.
Write because you
love to do something.
If you write for money,
you won't write anything
worth reading.'

Ray Bradbury

Haruki Murakami
The role of music

Writing office, Tokyo

Haruki Murakami (1949–) writes in an office on the sixth floor of a nondescript building in the Aoyama district of Tokyo. The most striking thing about the fairly simple space is that it is filled with 10,000 vinyl records, mainly jazz, covering a whole wall. Murakami usually listens to music while he writes. Indeed, he has talked about the commonalities between music and writing, and the four pillars of rhythm, melody, harmony and free improvisation.

Murakami began writing while he was running a Tokyo jazz club. He used an Olivetti typewriter and initially only managed to fit it in after the club shut in the early hours. Now his writing routine starts at his desk at about 4 a.m., with him concentrating intensely for five or six hours while he sips coffee. He exercises in the afternoon, running and/or swimming, then reads or listens to music – he says it gives him energy to write – before going to bed at 9 p.m.

His desk has various memorabilia dotted around it, including a wooden foot with a spider engraved on it (acquired on a trip to Laos), a marble sculpture with a wasp on top (from Scandinavia), a cat sculpture, a simple coffee mug (from Switzerland – it has the country's flag on it), a paperweight with an Alfred Knopf logo design (from New York) and a container in the shape of a huge peanut. He calls all of these his 'talismans'.

He writes with well-sharpened yellow pencils, gathered in glasses covered with reproductions of the album covers for *Cookin' with the Miles Davis Quintet* and *Relaxin' with the Miles Davis Quintet*, gifts from a record shop where he is a regular customer. The mouse mat design is a Moomintrolls comic strip and elsewhere on the desk there is a figurine of baseball pitcher Yasuhiro Ogawa (Murakami is a keen follower of the sport).

George Orwell
The limits of seclusion

Bedroom, Jura, Inner Hebrides

In May 1946, after a period of prolonged illness and overwork in London, George Orwell (1903–50) decided to take drastic action. With the aim of concentrating on his next novel, *Nineteen Eighty-Four*, he decided to self-isolate himself and his young son Richard on the island of Jura in the Inner Hebrides in Scotland. At this point, the working title for the book was 'The Last Man in Europe' and in his outline for the book, Orwell wrote about the 'loneliness of the writer. His feeling of being *the last man*'. What Orwell wanted was simply the peace to write. 'A writer's work is done at home and if he lets it happen he will be subjected to almost constant interruption,' he wrote in 'The Cost of Letters'.

On Jura, he lived and worked at a farmhouse called Barnhill on the north of the island, which had a population of around 300. Post arrived two or three times a week, the nearest neighbour was a mile away, and there was no telephone within 20 miles. The main connection to the outside world was Orwell's battery-operated radio. He did encourage visitors to come, but conditions for getting there, then staying there, did not encourage many to make the effort – there was no electricity, no hot water and only very basic transport. In fact, Orwell wrote nothing for three months, concentrating instead on what amounted to farming a smallholding (though he did build some bookshelves), using his real name, Eric Blair.

It was not a comfortable existence, a physically tough and austere lifestyle which mirrored the novel he was writing, and the cold and damp were hardly ideal for a tuberculosis sufferer. While Orwell was deeply attracted to life on the island – his diaries for his time on Jura read more like extensive nature notes and barely mention writing at all – he found it hard to work while he was ill, recording in his journal: 'It is only when you attempt to write … that you realize what a deterioration has

Orwell wrote in spartan conditions and remote surroundings on Jura.

happened inside your skull ... you cannot concentrate for more than a few seconds, and therefore cannot even remember what you said a moment ago.'

Orwell started off with just a camp bed, a table, a couple of chairs and basic kitchen utensils, but gradually increased his possessions. Once he got into a working routine, he usually wrote or typed most of the day, breaking off only for mealtimes or for a walk after dinner. Visitors reported he was happier talking about the flora and fauna of the island rather than his novel, although they heard him typing away in his room. In Michael Shelden's biography of Orwell, he describes the set-up: 'Barnhill would be not only his farmhouse but his office, his restaurant, his pub, his inn, and there would be few reminders of the outside world of wars, dirty streets, modern factories, and power politics.'

It was not a comfortable existence, a physically tough and austere lifestyle which mirrored the novel he was writing, and the cold and damp were hardly ideal for a tuberculosis sufferer.

From time to time Orwell wrote in his sitting room but chiefly in the big attic room on an untidy desk, and in his bedroom (often in his dressing gown) on an old Remington Home Portable typewriter, typing up his manuscript himself in the absence of any help, increasingly weak and sometimes coughing up blood as he went along. Occasionally he balanced the typewriter on his knees as he pounded away. He chain-smoked black shag roll-up cigarettes, drank plenty of tea and black coffee, and kept himself warm with a small paraffin heater. He wrote to David Astor, editor of the *Observer*, who had leant him the use of Barnhill, that: 'I have got so used to writing in bed that I think I prefer it, though of course it's awkward to type there.' He increasingly found it impossible to sit up in bed and type neatly for any length of time.

Sadly, while *Nineteen Eighty-Four* was an instant hit, Orwell's health declined rapidly and he was forced to leave Jura in early 1949 and died the following year.

Sylvia Plath
Domestic rooms with a view

Various sitting rooms, London and North Tawton, Devon

American writer Sylvia Plath (1932–63) mixed her career as a poet and novelist with a domestic routine that few male writers could match. Her days were spent on childcare and housework, including cookery which was a particular passion (she was very proud of her lemon meringue pie), fitting her writing in where and when she could. 'I have been working like mad,' she wrote to her mother in April 1961, 'and find if I just have five hours to write from 8–1 I can do all my housework and business during the rest of the day with a serene mind.'

The lack of a personal space to write was evident from the beginning of her controversial marriage to poet Ted Hughes, whose career she also dedicated herself to. While they were on honeymoon in Spain in 1956, Plath wrote a letter to her mother describing the table in the dining room which she and Hughes wrote on side by side – his side extremely messy with paper everywhere with an open bottle of blue ink on top of piles of papers, hers neat and tidy with books and notebooks lined up next to sunglasses, seashells and a pair of scissors (plus her bottle of black ink, the top tightly closed). In her homes with Hughes, she often wrote in their sitting room, sometimes putting a portable electric fire by her feet to warm them while she worked.

Before Plath had children, she and Hughes aimed to work in the morning from around 8.30 a.m. to noon, and then in the late afternoon from 4 p.m. to 6 p.m. Later, they shared childcare, Plath writing in the morning and Hughes in the afternoon. She wrote on pink memorandum paper and used a number of typewriters, a Royal as a student, a Smith-Corona, an Olivetti Lettera 22 (a present from her mother) and finally a light green Hermes 3000, which she used for her novel *The Bell Jar*.

When, at the end of August 1961, they moved to their rural Court Green home in North Tawton, Devon, their first spacious

Plath's days were a hectic mixture of writing and childcare.

home together, Plath finally managed to create her own writing room on the first floor, where she wrote in the mornings while Hughes looked after their daughter Frieda. It had two windows, one of which looked out to the neighbouring thirteenth-century church of St Peter's and the ancient yew tree she wrote about in several of her poems, including 'Little Fugue' ('The yew's black fingers wag; cold clouds go over') and 'The Moon and the Yew Tree'.

Various poems from her posthumous *Ariel* collection were written at Court Green on a large desk, 7ft (2m) long and 2.5ft (75cm) wide, made by her brother Warren and Hughes. On 15 September 1961, she wrote to her mother that it was 'an immense elm plank which will make me my first real capacious writing table'. Hughes also wrote about preparing it in his melancholy poem 'The Table' ('I wanted to make you a solid writing-table/That would last a lifetime.'). He describes 'The wild bark surfing along one edge of it/Rough-cut for coffin timber', on which she worked while drinking her morning Nescafé.

> On 15 September 1961, she wrote to her mother that it was 'an immense elm plank which will make me my first real capacious writing table'.

It was on this plank that on 12 October 1962, after Hughes had left her, Plath wrote her most famous poem, 'Daddy', while her children were still asleep, a method also adoped by American writer Toni Morrison. 'I am up at 5 writing the best poems of my life,' she wrote to her mother the same month, 'they will make my name.' In keeping with her interest in furnishing her homes attractively, Plath also liked to keep her working space pleasant and around the same time recorded that she had bright red late poppies and blue-purple cornflowers – which inspired her poem 'Poppies in October' – in a vase on her desk.

In December 1962, Plath and the children moved to a flat in Fitzroy Road in London where poet W.B. Yeats had lived and where her bedroom doubled as her study. Here she effectively lived and worked as a single mother, waking up around 4 a.m. to 5 a.m. to work on *Ariel* until her children woke up.

Beatrix Potter
A stage set for books

Bedroom, Near Sawrey, Cumbria

Beatrix Potter (1866–1943) bought the seventeenth-century Hill Top in Near Sawrey, Cumbria, in 1905, after the runaway success of *The Tale of Peter Rabbit*; she wrote thirteen of her books there.

Potter did not actually live at Hill Top – she lived nearby at Castle Farm – but used it entirely as a writing retreat, especially the upstairs bedroom, where she worked at a small wooden desk facing the window. Peter Rabbit grew out of sketches in letters to friends' children. Potter produced a dummy copy and published it privately in 1901 with a print run of 250 after half a dozen publishing houses initially turned it down, largely because she insisted on the size of the book being small enough for a child's hands and that the text should not rhyme.

Publishers Frederick Warne then took the book on and sold more than 20,000 copies in three months. Even after this made her name, she returned to self-publishing for *The Tailor of Gloucester* (1903). Potter also drove the early merchandizing of her works, designing and patenting a Peter Rabbit doll in 1903. Subsequent tea sets, wallpaper, stationery and other Potter products were all closely supervised by the author.

Even without visiting Hill Top, you can familiarize yourself with much of the layout of the house from the stories, including the entrance hall's stone-flagged floor, the eighteenth-century bannisters, and dresser (*The Tale of Samuel Whiskers*), and the dolls' house and furnishings (*The Tale of Two Bad Mice*).

Potter was a keen gardener and planned the layout of the garden herself. The flowers and shrubs can be seen particularly clearly in *The Tale of Tom Kitten*, used as a planting guide by the gardeners who look after it today. The book also features her white wicket gate, stone wall and lovely views from Hill Top across the countryside. Similar views of the garden and surrounding area are featured in *The Tale of Jemima Puddle-Duck*.

Potter stipulated that Hill Top must be left unchanged and untouched after her death, or as she put it in her will 'as if I had just gone out and they [visitors] had just missed me'.

Marcel Proust
The attraction of bed

Bedroom, Paris

Proust often suffered with cramped wrists after long writing sessions in bed.

While most writers tend to be fairly vertical when working, others have found a more relaxed approach equally attractive. Truman Capote described himself as a 'completely horizontal author' who could not think unless he was lying down on a bed or couch, while Mark Twain wrote about happily sitting up in bed with his pipe and scribbling away on a board. But leading the bed-based brigade is Marcel Proust, whose major work *The Remembrance of Things Past* begins 'For a long time, I went to bed early'.

In 1906, shortly after his parents died, Proust (1871–1922) moved into an apartment at the Boulevard Haussmann in Paris. He had found it very hard to cope with their deaths and had problems sleeping. His solution was to isolate himself in his bedroom, where he developed a largely nocturnal schedule, sleeping during the day and writing at night.

It was quite a capacious room with 12ft- (3.7m-) high ceilings, previously owned by his uncle. Here, Proust cocooned himself using shutters and heavy satin curtains to help prevent pollen and outside dust contamination from bringing on his asthma. Additionally, he wanted to keep his work space as quiet as possible (although he kept his telephone for a while, this also eventually had to go) and, on the advice of his friend the poet Anna de Noailles, he had the walls and ceiling lined with cork. Initially he intended to wallpaper them, but never got round to it, and over the years they darkened from the fumes of the medicinal powders he burnt against his asthma.

Even this was not sufficient to maintain the standard of silence he was after. Proust's letters to the neighbours – Mme Marie Williams and her husband, Charles (a dentist whose chair lay directly above Proust's bedroom) – are both extraordinarily polite while at the same time full of variations on the theme of 'please keep the noise down'.

Wrapped up on his simple bed in jumpers and surrounded by hot water bottles, Proust wrote half-sitting-up, his knees substituting as a kind of desk. His housekeeper Céleste Albaret, who provided him with his daily croissants and top-ups of hot coffee, said she never saw him write even a note standing. He wrote in lined notebooks, with double-lined red margins. It was not a wholly comfortable position and long writing sessions sometimes left him with cramped wrists.

The room itself was surprisingly cluttered, which lessened the tomb-like effect. While Proust's bed was tucked into a corner as far away from the window as possible, he kept three tables close by him for his writing needs, including his green-shaded bedside lamp, and other necessities, such as a bottle of Evian water. Further away, standing on the parquet floor, was his mother's piano, his father's library armchair and revolving bookcases, and a writing desk that Proust never used, all with happy emotional associations with his parents, even if unremarkable pieces in design terms. (A possibly apocryphal story has Oscar Wilde meeting Proust's parents and exclaiming 'How ugly your house is!'.) Elsewhere were oriental-style items: a screen, cabinet and rug. There were no paintings and the only decoration was a small white statuette of the young Jesus. Two mirrors were sited so that he could not see himself while in bed. It was not exactly spartan, but it was something of a blank canvas and there were effectively no distractions to lure him away from his writing, work he saw as his patriotic duty.

Proust's letters to the neighbours are both extraordinarily polite while at the same time full of variations on the theme of 'please keep the noise down'.

It is not clear exactly why Proust chose to write in bed. While the contents of Proust's room suggest he found comfort in the familiarity of objects which had connections to loved ones, maybe he required somewhere that was both intimate and uniquely his own to stimulate his writing. 'It is pleasant, when one is distraught, to lie in the warmth of one's bed,' he wrote as a young man in his first book *Les plaisirs et les jours* (*Pleasures and Regrets*,

1896), 'and there, with all effort and struggle at an end, even perhaps with one's head under the blankets, surrender completely to howling, like branches in the autumn wind.'

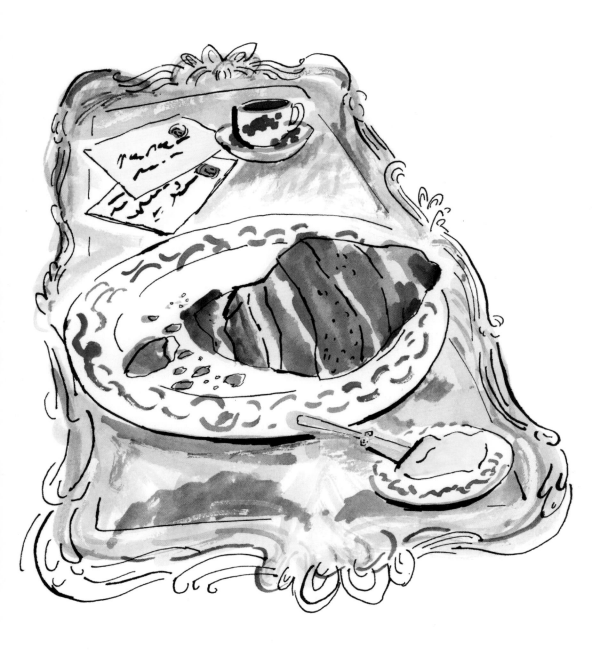

J.K. Rowling
The importance of a good café

Various cafés, Edinburgh

Cafés provided J.K. Rowling (1965–) with an important – and cheap – working space to write her early Harry Potter books, with her young daughter asleep in a buggy next to her as she wrote.

According to Rowling, Edinburgh is where Harry evolved over hours of writing in its cafés, partly because it meant she didn't have to make her own coffee, but also because she enjoyed being surrounded by other people rather than writing alone. It also afforded her the chance to move location from café to café when she needed a fresh atmosphere to inspire her. Her ideal location was a café which was reasonably busy, but not so much that she had to share a table. *Harry Potter and the Philospher's Stone* was written between the Traverse Theatre Café on Cambridge Street and the corner table in Nicolson's Café (now Spoon), where her regular order was an espresso and a glass of water. But her preferred spot for the second and third volumes of the series was the back room of the Elephant House on George IV Bridge, which has views over Edinburgh Castle.

Though she still writes in longhand, writing in public is obviously no longer an option. Instead, she has found inspiration in other places, including hotel rooms. She completed the final Harry Potter book in Room 552, or what is now known as the J.K. Rowling Suite in the Balmoral Hotel, Edinburgh, where she hid herself away to finish the adventures in the Deathly Hallows. To mark the event, she signed and dedicated a marble bust of Hermes (still in situ), while the hotel has since added an owl doorknocker.

More recently she has worked in an office in her back garden, where she has numerous cups of tea and non-messy snacks like popcorn while listening mostly to classical music to avoid the distraction of human voices.

Rowling is among the many writers who have found inspiration in cafés.

Vita Sackville-West
A room to celebrate love(s)

Tower, Sissinghurst Castle, Kent

When novelist, journalist, poet and gardener Vita Sackville-West (1892–1962) moved to the largely dilapidated sixteenth-century Sissinghurst Castle in Kent with her husband Harold Nicolson in 1930, the first building she restored was the imposingly tall tower. This fairy-tale building was what first attracted her to the property, since it reminded her of her ancestral home at nearby Knole, which, as a woman, she was ineligible to inherit.

The tower room above the archway became her writing room: 'the high room where tall the shadows tilt', as she described it in her 1930 poem 'Sissinghurst'. She employed local builders to construct oak bookshelves and a corner fireplace and to turn a turret into an octagonal library. Sissinghurst provided her with a refuge from the world and its accepted social norms and she kept this writing space for herself, rarely allowing anybody to enter. She wrote at an oak desk facing a seventeenth-century Flemish tapestry, with light provided by a high, latticed window to her right. There were Persian rugs on the floor and a good-sized daybed in dark olive elephant cord. On the windowsills she arranged shells and pebbles collected on her travels.

Vita filled the room with a variety of objects associated with her lovers: a pair of Chinese crystal rabbits and a red lava ring (a gift from Violet Trefusis), lovely calligraphy work (a poem about the delights of Kent by seventeenth-century poet Phineas Fletcher, produced by Christopher St John, formerly Christabel Marshall), and embroidery (by Gwen St Aubyn, a photo of whom was also on her writing desk). More of St John's work was hung on a nearby wall: 'To The Love of his CONSTANT HEART', an anonymous poem from the first printed poetry anthology, *Tottel's Miscellany* of 1557.

On her writing desk, next to her reproduction of Branwell Brontë's paintings of his sisters and a small engraving of Knole, was a photograph of Harold. Opposite it was another, taken in

Sackville-West wrote in her tower for three decades and never redecorated.

1929 by society photographer Lenare, of her most famous lover, Virginia Woolf, whose 1928 novel *Orlando* she had inspired. Elsewhere on the desk she kept various notebooks detailing which books she had lent to friends, her garden accounts and transcriptions of her dreams. She painted the cabinet just above her desk a striking bronze green.

In her library turret she also kept a black Gladstone bag containing her writings about Violet. These formed the basis of the hugely successful 1973 book *Portrait of a Marriage* by her son Nigel (he had to slash it open after her death because he couldn't unlock it).

Harold and Vita's libraries at Sissinghurst numbered 11,000 books, and around 2,700 were in her private writing space. Her collection was particularly strong on gardening, travel, sex and twenty-four books by Virginia Woolf, including a dedication copy of *Orlando*. The poetry of W.B. Yeats, Stephen Spender, T.S. Eliot and Edith Sitwell was well represented.

The tower room above the archway became her writing room: 'the high room where tall the shadows tilt', as she described it in her 1930 poem 'Sissinghurst'.

Over the thirty years she worked in the tower – writing at night after working in the garden during the day – she never redecorated it. The only time she stopped writing there was during the Second World War, moving out during the winter of 1941–2 because coal was hard to get, which left the space too cold. She returned in April 1945.

Sissinghurst Castle is in fact home to another impressive writer's room. Next to the moat is Nigel's writing gazebo, with lovely views over the surrounding countryside. He built it in 1969 as a memorial to his father and wrote *Portrait of a Marriage* inside, even while tourists in the garden were milling around outside. It had no telephone, no lighting and no heating. Intriguingly, it is built to the same specifications as the Apollo 11 lunar module, which also happily coincides with the typical oast architecture of the area. A project is under way to restock the shelves with the same editions of the books he worked with, including the works of Jane Austen, and histories and maps of Kent.

George Bernard Shaw
Writing room as branding tool

Writing hut, Ayot St Lawrence, Hertfordshire

A writer's room tends to be a private place, a sanctuary from domesticity and the excitements of children, pets and unwanted visitors. This is certainly how George Bernard Shaw (1856–1920) promoted his writing hut to the world, with himself as something of a creative hermit, tucked away in his modest retreat with only a few pens, a supply of ink, a small table, a narrow bed and a wicker chair for comfort. His biographer Michael Holroyd described it as a kind of 'monk's cell'. The truth is a little more complicated.

Shaw's writing refuge was a 65sq ft (6m²) wooden summerhouse, originally intended for his wife Charlotte and inspired by the similar set-up owned by his neighbour, Apsley Cherry-Garrard, the naturalist who was part of Scott's expedition to the Antarctic. The hut at his home in Shaw's Corner, Ayot St Lawrence, Hertfordshire, was built on a revolving base that used castors on a circular track. This meant that it could be rotated to improve the light or change the view (or indeed just for a bit of exercise). Spectacularly high-tech for its time, it also had an electric heater and a telephone connection to the house, as well as an alarm clock to alert the Nobel Prize winner to lunchtime. Shaw particularly enjoyed the isolation, since it allowed the staff at the house with some degree of honesty to tell callers that 'Mr Shaw is out' to prevent interruptions. He also called it 'London' for the same reasons ('I'm sorry Sir, Mr Shaw is in London').

'Any place that will hold a bed and a writing table is as characteristic of me as any other,' Shaw said in an interview for *The World* magazine in July 1900. But this apparent indifference to his writing space belies the way in which he used the hut as a real-life stage to promote his ideas and beliefs.

As a journalist as well as a playwright, and generally prolific writer, Shaw had a keen appreciation of the power of photography as used within mass media, keeping press cuttings about himself

GBS's aged shed, the kind of writing space many writers dream about, can still be seen in the grounds of his house.

in special albums. He was certainly not a monk in terms of worldliness. A friend of the US press baron William Randolph Hearst, Shaw ensured that glimpses of his own life were always stage-managed to create a specific impression, playing on his reputation as a media celebrity at a time when there was growing interest in the private lives of famous people.

It was also a time when there was growing interest in the concept of 'rusticity', a delight in the rural idyll, with a knock-on effect for installing garden buildings. Shaw made the most of this movement, promoting himself as a reclusive thinker toiling in his rural shelter, bothered by intrusions from press and people alike, while at the same time inviting in newspapers and magazines for whom he posed for photos.

Thus, in August 1929, Shaw appeared with his hut in *Modern Mechanics and Inventions* magazine, promoting the idea of sunlight as a healing agent. The dramatic poses he effected for these shots were in line with his interest in eurhythmics, the concept of developing the body in harmony. He also had special Vitaglass windows installed, a move which was also picked up by newspapers, and his ownership of a hut on a turntable placed him in the vanguard of medical thought, since rotating summerhouses were used to treat people suffering from tuberculosis. Not all his campaigns linked to the outdoors featured his hut; Shaw was a supporter of nudism, but always publicized the hut fully clothed.

And of course he used the shed to show off his celebrity friends. In spring 1944, when the actress Vivian Leigh was in London shooting a film version of Shaw's play *Caesar & Cleopatra* with her husband Laurence Oliver, she took advantage of the proximity of Shaw's home in Hertfordshire to visit him with the film's flamboyant director Gabriel Pascal. Naturally, there were promotional photographs of her visit, taken by Wilfrid Newton. There is also video footage from 1949 of comedian and actor Danny Kaye visiting Shaw at home in his garden.

> *His ownership of a hut on a turntable placed him in the vanguard of medical thought, since rotating summerhouses were used to treat people suffering from tuberculosis.*

Zadie Smith
Keeping the internet at bay

Various small rooms, New York

English novelist and creative writing professor Zadie Smith (1975–) is not hung up on the idea of a dedicated writing room, though she has been lucky enough to inherit E.L. Doctorow's old office at New York University where she teaches, and often writes there.

Her only real requirement is a small room with not much natural light, a dimness which she can produce using blinds. This is a constraint dictated partly by her day job and also by the requirements of her children's school pickup. So on days when she is not teaching, this has meant a 9 a.m. to 2.30 p.m. routine. Importantly, rather than limiting her time online, Smith works on a computer that is completely disconnected from the internet (she is not a fan of social media).

She does not write every day and says her imperative to write is a feeling of urgency, so if she does not feel compelled to write, she doesn't. When in the middle of a new work, she begins by rereading what she has already written, then deciding where edits are needed before writing fresh material. This makes for a slow process but one which does not require additional drafts when it is finished. A huge percentage of her time is spent on the initial fifty pages of the book, to ensure she gets it exactly how she wants it, the rest following at rapid speed.

Smith's desk is covered in novels of a wide range of genres so she can easily pick up something to provide a varied literary diet. Following this approach, she describes using 'Kafka as roughage' and turning to Dostoyevsky as 'the patron saint of substance over style'. The only requirement is that, while she is writing, the choice of novels has to be of high quality, with more 'comfort food' reading left for another time.

She also likes to have an inspirational quote to hand. One of her most recent is from philosopher Jacques Derrida: 'If a right to a secret is not maintained then we are in a totalitarian space.'

Smith: No social media, no distractions.

Danielle Steel
The delights of the desk

Study, Paris and San Francisco

Best-selling romantic novelist Danielle Steel (1947–) writes in her homes in Paris and San Francisco, her walls decorated with framed covers of her books and favourite encouraging sayings, including 'There are no miracles. There is only discipline', 'What hath night to do with sleep?' (John Milton) and 'Only a life lived for others is a life worthwhile' (attributed to Albert Einstein).

Her home in San Francisco is also home to her remarkable desk, an imposing bespoke build in the shape of three of her bestsellers: *Star*, *Daddy* and *Heartbeat*. Steel's routine is quite spectacular, working long hours every day at her desk to produce half a dozen new novels every year. Starting at 8.30 a.m. in her cashmere nightgown, she has a slice of toast and an iced decaff coffee, works until lunch, snacks on bittersweet chocolate in the afternoon and often finishes very late at night or early the following morning. She writes on a 1946 Olympia standard typewriter, which she calls 'Olly'. (In fact, there have been a dozen Ollys over the years, still carefully kept for parts.)

Interestingly, although Steel is very keen on interior design, the desk's designers chose both the book titles and the colours, white for *Star*, a bright red for *Heartbeat* and a deep blue for *Daddy*. She is also very practical when it comes to her desk, which has numerous objects her children have given her as good luck totems, including artwork, magnets and a nameplate which belonged to her late son, Nick, with the name of his punk band Link 80 on it. 'They touch my heart,' she says, 'but do not help my creative process. The desktop is so crowded that, when I'm writing, I have to take them off the desk until I finish the book.'

Steel works on one of the most wonderful desks in the world.

'It has become increasingly plain to me that the very excellent organization of a long book or the finest perceptions and judgment in time of revision do not go well with liquor.'

F. Scott Fitzgerald

'Throw up into your typewriter every morning.
Clean up every noon.'

Raymond Chandler

Gertrude Stein
Cows and cars

Cars in various rural locations

John Steinbeck turned the back seat of his Ford station wagon into a writing space, with a folding desk and room for all his writing equipment and coffee. Vladamir Nabakov wrote many of his notes for *Lolita* in his car. And likewise, avant-garde writer Gertrude Stein (1874–1946) found automobiles inspirational.

American-born but mostly Paris-based, Stein was very keen on cars, driving herself and her partner Alice B. Toklas in Model T Fords which she nicknamed 'Auntie' (after her Aunt Pauline) and 'Godiva' (because of its sparse dashboard). Stein did all the driving and when she parked up on shopping trips would write in the passenger seat while Toklas went off with the bags. She even wrote her essay on writing technique 'Composition as Explanation' while sitting in a Ford car while her car was being repaired.

Stein's best-known book, *The Autobiography of Alice B. Toklas* (1933), emphasizes how much she was inspired by the sounds of crowded streets and especially 'the movement of the automobiles', which she found liberating while writing at speed. The book also compares her writing process to the non-stop factory production of cars. 'In the Twentieth Century you feel like movement,' she wrote.

Sometimes the car trips would take the couple far from the famous Saturday-night salon they hosted at their home into the countryside. Here, they would apparently drive around until they found a spot for Stein to write, selected for its view of cows (associated in Stein's writings with orgasms) and rocks. Stein would write on a campstool with pencil and paper until she felt she needed a new cow to motivate her, at which point Toklas would either steer one into sight or they would get in the car and drive off to find another. These writing sessions were each only about a quarter of an hour long and Stein said she only wrote about 30 minutes a day in total.

John Steinbeck
Pencils maketh the writing room

Writing hut, Long Island, New York; apartment, New York

In a 1958 letter to his friend and agent Elizabeth Otis, American novelist John Steinbeck (1902–68) outlined his plans for building what he described as his 'little lighthouse', somewhere that was too small for a bed so that it could never be used as a guest room. 'It will be off limits to everyone,' he told her. 'One of its main features will be an imposing padlock on the door.'

Steinbeck's writing hut on Long Island, New York, was so dear to him that he actually gave it a name, Joyous Garde (he even hand-made a sign for it and stuck it above the door outside). Named after Sir Lancelot's castle, the hexagonal structure at Sag Harbor was inspired by Mark Twain's own garden office and enjoyed marvellous views over the cove near Bluff Point. The attractive hut with windows in every wall was built by Steinbeck himelf and he worked inside in a director's chair which he labelled 'Siege Perilous' – indeed, Joyous Garde had only one chair, so visitors had nowhere to sit down. A large desk took up much of the room, allowing him to spread papers and books out, and a bookshelf ran all round the room over the windows. In this cosy abode, which he initially planned to call Sanity's Stepchild, he wrote his travelogue *Travels with Charley* and his final novel *Winter of Our Discontent*.

As well as Joyous Garde, Steinbeck enjoyed the peace of the writing room in his apartment on the Upper East Side of New York City, which he described as 'a quiet room where nothing ever happens'. It was so quiet, in fact, that he talked about getting a mynah bird and teaching it to ask him questions. He had a sign on the outside of the door which read 'Buzzard's Despair' and on the reverse 'Tidy Town', which is how his wife adjusted it to show she had been in and tidied it while he was out.

But whichever writing room he worked in, Steinbeck – who liked to write rapidly – had one prerequisite: pencils, and plenty of them. 'I like the feeling of a pencil,' he said, which was something of an understatement. He used hundreds on each new book, sharpened to a point that his son Thom called 'surgical'. 'The pure luxury of long beautiful pencils charges me with energy and invention,' said Steinbeck. And his quest for the perfect pencil was never-ending. 'For years I have looked for the perfect pencil,' he once wrote. 'I have found very good ones, but never the perfect one. And all the time it was not the pencils but me. A pencil that is all right some days is no good another day.' He had soft writing days and hard writing days, according to pencils. Sometimes it changed in the middle of the day.

He was particularly keen on round pencils, as he found hexagonal ones cut into his fingers. Nevertheless, he wrote with them so often that he developed a grooved callus on his finger where the pencil rested. Another requirement was that they be black so that they did not distract him. Favourite brands included the Blaisdell Calculator 600, the Eberhard Faber Mongol 480 and the Eberhard Faber Blackwing 602.

Steinbeck also had an electric sharpener of which he was very fond, calling it his most used and most useful possession. Since he began each morning with a wooden box of twenty-four fully sharpened pencils which he rotated and resharpened during the day, it was certainly a great help.

Steinbeck acknowledged that this love of pencils, what he called his 'pencil trifling', was one of his eccentricities. But he had others. He wrote his novel *East of Eden* on the right-hand pages of

a book, while using the left-hand ones to compose letters to his friend and editor Pascal Covici about the progress of the book, as well as general news. In fact, he started his morning work with the letter to warm up – Steinbeck explained he felt the need to 'have to dawdle a certain amount before I go to work'.

Despite this low-tech obsession, Steinbeck was actually keen to make use of new technology, using a Dictaphone to try out dialogue for his novels and typing up manuscripts on his olive green Hermes Baby typewriter, one of the earliest portables. On its case he scratched 'The Beast Within'.

Wordcounts

Writers' targets for their daily tally vary tremendously, even during their own careers. At one end of the scale was Graham Greene, who hit 500 a day, while J.G. Ballard aimed for double that, and Frederick Forsyth has estimated his output at twelve pages or 3,000 words a day. Lee Child regards 600 daily words as a minimum, twice that as fine, and four times that marking a great day.

Anthony Trollope, author of *Barchester Towers* and *The Way We Live Now*, described himself as a 'literary labourer' and suggested that 'three hours a day will produce as much as a man ought to write'. But he worked intensively during those three hours. 'It had at this time become my custom,' he wrote in his autobiobraphy, 'and it still is my custom, though of late I have become a little lenient to myself, to write with my watch before me, and to require from myself 250 words every quarter of an hour. I have found that the 250 words

have been forthcoming as regularly as my watch went.'

Mark Twain wrote in his autobiography that as a young man he could average 3,000 words a day. This dipped towards the end of the twentieth century. 'In 1897, when we were living in Tedworth Square, London,' he wrote, 'and I was writing the book called *Following the Equator*, my average was 1,800 words a day; here in Florence (1904) my average seems to be 1,400 words per sitting of four or five hours.'

However, getting stuck up on a specific figure may not be ideal. John Steinbeck suggested forgetting about any kind of target and simply writing a page a day. Ernest Hemingway also advised not to write too much at a single sitting and 'never pump yourself dry'. Or as Lewis Carroll put it: 'only go on working so long as the brain is *quite* clear. The moment you feel the ideas getting confused leave off and rest.'

Dylan Thomas
The appeal of small rooms in Wales

Writing shed, Laugharne, Wales

In a BBC broadcast in 1949, for which he recited some of his poems, Dylan Thomas explained how he had made the selection. He had omitted those he felt were 'pretty peculiar' but included those he was happiest with 'when, in small rooms in Wales, arrogantly and devotedly, I began them'.

Thomas (1914–53) certainly found inspiration in compact spaces. He wrote in a caravan at the end of the garden while living in a flat in Delancey Street in London; produced most of his *Portrait of the Artist as a Young Dog* in a summerhouse in the grounds of Laugharne Castle in Wales; enjoyed the use of a summerhouse at Magdalen College in Oxford provided by his patron Margaret Taylor; and was pleased to write in the 'Apple House' outbuilding at Llanina Mansion near New Quay, Wales, owned by Lord Howard de Walden.

The most famous of his writing rooms was his last: a former garage in Laugharne built in the 1920s to house the local doctor's green Wolseley, the first car in the town. It stands on cast-iron stilts, cantilevered off the road and jutting out beyond the cliff where it overlooks the Tâf estuary below. In 1949 it was converted into a writing shed for Thomas while he and his wife Caitlin moved into their nearby home known as the Boathouse, paid for again by Margaret Taylor. 'All I shall write in this water and tree room on the cliff, every word will be my thanks to you,' Thomas wrote in a letter to her.

The shed was very much Thomas's personal sanctuary. He had windows and a stove installed, and decorated it with pictures of his favourite writers (Louis MacNeice, Lord Byron, Walt Whitman, W.H. Auden and D.H. Lawrence), lists of words and reproductions of art including Botticelli's *The Birth of Venus* and Pieter Bruegel the Elder's *The Peasant Wedding*. As well as piles of paper on his desk (its legs painted red), he also liked to keep his favourite boiled sweets

Thomas wrote in the shed, with regular visits to Brown's Hotel for a drink during the day.

close at hand. There were also shelves of books, although Caitlin is said to have taken out the Raymond Chandlers and other thrillers to encourage him to concentrate rather than settle in for a comfy read. Here, he wrote out everything by hand, simply throwing unwanted drafts onto the floor.

'My study, atelier, or bard's bothy, roasts on a cliff-top,' wrote Dylan Thomas in a letter to his friend Hector MacIver. From this peak, it certainly afforded him fine views across Carmarthen Bay and to the Llansteffan peninsula. Through the windows he could also see Sir John's Hill, which features in his eponymous poem ('Over Sir John's hill/The hawk on fire hangs still'). The shed itself features most dramatically in his 'Poem on His Birthday' to mark his thirty-fifth, which starts 'In his house on stilts high among beaks/And palavers of birds' and goes on to describe the author as 'the rhymer in the long tongued room'.

Thomas also wrote 'Do Not Go Gentle into That Good Night' and parts of *Under Milk Wood* here.

His normal writing routine was as simple as his shed. In the morning he would read, write letters or complete crossword puzzles, go for for a drink around midday at the local Brown's Hotel, return for lunch at 1 p.m., then work in the shed from 2 p.m. until 7 p.m, and then return to Brown's with Caitlin for the evening. To encourage him to work, Caitlin sometimes locked him in the shed.

The shed has remained popular long after Thomas's death. It motivated Roald Dahl to build his own writing hut to exactly the same proportions (see page 54) following a family trip to Wales, a recreation featured in the 2011 Chelsea Flower Show and a pop-up replica version of the writing shed went on the road in England and Wales to mark Thomas's 100th birthday. After falling into disrepair, it was renovated in 2003 at a cost of £20,000 (it had cost £5 to build) and the interior is a recreation of his working environment, alongside empty beer bottles, his blue-and-white striped mug (copies of which are now on sale by an enterprising Welsh pottery company) and a jacket over the back of the chair.

Mark Twain
The lure of the billiard room (and shed)

Billiard room, Hartford, Connecticut; writing shed, Elmira, New York

Like most writers, Mark Twain (1835–1910) preferred to work in the peace of his own sanctuary, but in his case he also mixed business with pleasure by writing in the same room as the billiard table on which he spent many happy hours playing by himself and with friends. 'It was plain that I had worked myself out, pumped myself dry,' he wrote to his Edinburgh-based friend Dr John Brown in September 1874, 'So I knocked off, and went to playing billiards for a change.'

This billiard/writing room was on the top floor of his three-storey red-brick house in Hartford, Connecticut. Although light and roomy, with plenty of windows, Twain wrote at a desk facing a wall to minimize distractions (the current urban view would have been a far lovelier rural one in his day). Next to his desk, usually fairly cluttered with papers, was a shelving unit with various compartments where he kept his drafts. He used the billiard table to spread out his manuscripts before editing them.

> '*When the storms sweep down the remote valley and the lightning flashes above the hills beyond, and the rain beats upon the roof over my head, imagine the luxury of it!*'

Twain also wrote in an octagonal shed built in 1874 at Quarry Farm, in Elmira, upstate New York, at the home of his sister-in-law Susan Crane. Here he would begin work after a hearty breakfast and stay inside, usually missing lunch, writing and smoking cigars until 5 p.m. Family and friends did not disturb him, blowing a horn to get his attention if he was needed up at the house. While his home in Hartford was something of a magnet for the literary world, his shed in Elmira where he worked every summer for two decades was a peaceful spot with far less going on.

Twain used his billiard table as an extended desk before turning to the quiet of a writing shed.

'Susie Crane has built me the loveliest study you ever saw,' he wrote to Reverend Joseph Twichell and his wife Harmony back in Hartford. 'It is octagonal with a peaked roof, each face filled with a spacious window and it sits perched in complete isolation on the top of an elevation that commands leagues of valley and city and retreating ranges of distant blue hills. It is a cosy nest, with just room in it for a sofa and a table and three or four chairs – and when the storms sweep down the remote valley and the lightning flashes above the hills beyond, and the rain beats upon the roof over my head, imagine the luxury of it!'

The study was 100 yards (90m) away from the house and about 12ft (3.7m) wide with cat flaps to allow his favourite pets to come in and out while he was writing. It had a brick fireplace and a desk but was not richly decorated inside. It has been likened to the kind of riverboat pilot house in which Twain worked as a young man and wrote about in his memoir *Life on the Mississippi*. 'On hot days,' he wrote to Dr Brown, 'I spread the study wide open, anchor my papers down with brickbats and write in the midst of the hurricanes, clothed in the same thin linen we make shirts of ... It is remote from all noises.'

Novelist John Steinbeck was one who agreed on the loveliness of Twain's sanctuary, using it as inspiration for his own hexagonal writing shed, which he named Joyous Garde (see page 155).

Kurt Vonnegut
A room of rejection

Study, West Barnstable, Massachusetts

At the Kurt Vonnegut Museum and Library in the writer's home town of Indianapolis in the US, there are objects from all parts of his life, and the museum has replicated his study from the time he lived in West Barnstable, Massachusetts. Visitors can see the framed photograph of his father which he hung in his work room, his Smith-Corona typewriter (he had a strong dislike of electronic ones) and the low coffee table on which it perched while the 6ft 2in (1.88m) writer hunched unergonomically over it producing *Breakfast of Champions*. Into this desk he carved a quote from Henry Thoreau's book *Walden* ('Beware of all enterprises that require new clothes') and on top of it stands his lamp in the shape of a red cockerel. There is also a packet of his favourite unfiltered Pall Mall cigarettes, which he lost behind the back of his bookcase and was found after his death.

The recreated space though also offers a look at the quirkier side of Vonnegut (1922–2007), since it contains the many rejection slips for his short stories from magazines, framed on the walls. He kept these in an old red box. Among them is one from *The Atlantic Monthly* in 1949 suggesting that his piece on the wartime destruction of Dresden – which he experienced first hand – was 'not quite compelling enough'. Another from *Collier's* magazine for his short story 'Mnemonics' says it 'is worked out in superficial and insufficient terms which make it flat and inconsequential'. Indeed, there were so many rejection letters that his wife Jane decorated a wastebasket with them.

One of Vonnegut's other writing idiosyncrasies was how he assembled his manuscripts. For his 1959 novel *The Sirens of Titan*, he stapled his typed-up drafts together to form long scrolls of text (a similar technique to Jack Kerouac's method for *On the Road*). Chapters are dozens of feet long, though only 8in (20cm) wide.

Vonnegut made his favourite motivational quote more permanent than a mere post-it note.

Edith Wharton
The comfort of pets

Bedroom, Lenox, Massachusetts

Wharton wrote from her bed to prevent interruptions (and to keep her beloved pets near at hand).

Judging by her publicity photos, the natural assumption would be that American novelist Edith Wharton (1862–1937) wrote in a traditional manner, at the gold-tooled leather-topped desk in her extremely well-stocked library. But while this looked quite natural, it was in fact a deliberate illusion. In fact, Wharton was at her most creative and most comfortable while writing in bed, a practice somewhat bizarrely recreated by a 2012 *Vogue* photoshoot in which Russian model Natalia Vodianova donned an Alberta Ferretti chiffon dress with crystal collar.

Although Wharton experimented with a typewriter, she much preferred to write by hand on her writing board, which was carefully fitted with an inkpot. She usually only wrote in the morning until around 11 a.m. or noon and her custom was to gently drop pages as she finished them on to the floor. These would be picked up later by servants and then typed up by her secretary and former governess Anna Bahlmann (played by Juno Temple in the *Vogue* shoot). Nobody was allowed to intrude on her writing space while she was working.

Wharton does refer to this bed-based set-up as a 'reprehensible habit' and recounts in her autobiography of an incident when she was staying at a friend's house and accidentally knocked the inkpot over, flooding the sheets black, well beyond the help of blotting paper (and then asking the maid not to mention it to the owners). 'Inkstands and tea-cups are never as full as when one upsets them,' she wrote.

Wharton was both knowledgeable and practical about schemes for domestic spaces and her 1897 book *The Decoration of Houses* was a popular success, and indeed is still in print. She designed her forty-two-room mansion the Mount in Lenox, Massachusetts, and put her bedroom and sitting room suite above the library to make sure it was quiet when she was working.

She recounts in her autobiography *A Backward Glance* that the house was essential to her work as it 'gave me the freedom from trivial obligations which was necessary if I was to go on with my writing'. Writing from her bed meant she could be comfortable (without company there was no need to wear a corset or other constricting clothing) and also put a stop to interruptions. Her friend and literary executor Gaillard Lapsley described what she typically wore: 'a thin silk sacque [gown] with loose sleeves, open at the neck and trimmed with lace and on her head a cap of the same material also trimmed with lace which fell about her brow and ears like the edging of a lamp shade'.

Her regime certainly worked. The Mount – named a National Historic Landmark in 1971 – was where she wrote her 1905 breakthrough novel *The House of Mirth* as well as numerous other successful titles including *Ethan Frome*. But her routine was not restricted to her home. One of Wharton's great loves was travel, and she was equally fastidious about the layout of her hotel rooms, ensuring that their staff place furniture just so for her morning writing sessions.

But there was another magic ingredient apart from the bed. Wharton also wrote with her much-loved dogs around her, closely relaxing on the bed, among the spread of books, newspapers and correspondence. Like many writers, she was a keen dog owner throughout her life, preferring Pekingese as she grew older including Linky (her favourite – Wharton died only four months after Linky in 1926).

Wharton claimed the dogs helped her cope with the challenges of life, a problematic marriage and divorce, as well as a nervous breakdown. As an indication of her devotion to them, she also built a pet cemetery for them at the Mount.

Pets

Although Norwegian autobiographist Karl Ove Knausgård has suggested that his family's pet dog prevented him from writing literary prose for two years, many pets have been welcomed by authors into their writing rooms and routines, such as writer and illustrator Edward Gorey, who allowed his half a dozen cats to sit on his desk as he drew. Other literary pets included:

Bobs – A fox terrier, who 'wrote' Enid Blyton's columns about home life for *Teacher's World* magazine (his death in 1935 did not stop his columns running for another decade).

Bounce – A female Great Dane, who relaxed at the feet of English poet and satirist Alexander Pope and acted as protection against writers Pope had mocked when she and her master went for a walk.

Catarina/Catterina – A tortoiseshell cat, which sat on Edgar Allan Poe's shoulder while he wrote and inspired his short story 'The Black Cat'.

Daffy – A grey tabby, to whom Lucy Maud Montgomery, author of the 'Anne of Green Gables' series for children, read drafts of her work.

Lola – Truman Capote's raven, who hid the first page of a short story he was writing, which he then had to abandon.

Luath – J.M. Barrie's white Landseer Newfoundland, who was the inspiration for Nana, the nursemaid dog in *Peter Pan*.

Sprite – Bill Watterson's cat, who was partly the inspiration for Hobbes in his Calvin and Hobbes cartoons.

Taki – Raymond Chandler's black Persian cat, who sat on his lap, his typewriter and his papers.

Toby – John Steinbeck's much loved Irish Setter, who unfortunately ate half of an early draft of *Of Mice and Men*.

Screenwriter and novelist Aldous Huxley believed humans and cats were quite alike. He advised aspiring writers who wanted an insight into the psychological mind of humans to keep a pair of cats, ideally Siamese, then watch them and take notes on their behaviour as research.

E.B. White
Keeping it simple

Writing shed, Allen Cove, Maine

Rather than fill his writing hut with momentoes of trips or family members, American writer E.B. White (1899–1985), famous for *Charlotte's Web* and *Stuart Little*, kept his starkly spartan.

It was not purpose-built as a writing studio, but was originally a boathouse. White remarked that it sheltered him better than his actual home, a late-eighteenth-century farmhouse, and that inside his shed he was a 'wilder and healthier man'. He wrote that he shared it with a mouse and a squirrel, and for a while foxes burrowed underneath it to make their own den.

The wooden shack at his coastal home in Allen Cove, Maine, New England, had a lovely view out to sea but was not fitted out in luxury. White had a chair, bench, desk (which he built himself), blue metal ashtray, a barrel as a wastebasket, a cupboard upcycled from a croquet set box and his black Underwood typewriter, which his caretaker would drive down to the shed in the morning and bring back in the evening. 'Tight and plainly finished,' was White's description of it. It was here that he wrote the first draft of *Charlotte's Web*, the farm on the property providing stimulation for the story while the initial impetus came directly from watching a spider spin an egg sac on the ceiling of his writing shed.

The idea of working in a small, detached space had an extra appeal for White. He loved the writings of the writer and naturalist Henry David Thoreau, especially *Walden*, his account of carving out a simple life in nature in his home-made cabin by a lake in Massachusetts. By happy chance, Thoreau's cabin was almost the same size as White's boathouse, 10ft by 15ft (3m by 4.6m). Writing inside must have been an additional inspiration for White as well as a pleasure.

White's simple shed helped to inspire *Charlotte's Web*.

P.G. Wodehouse
A healthy mind in a healthy body

Study, London and Long Island, New York

P.G. Wodehouse had a long and prolific career, writing hundreds of novels, short stories, musicals and plays. He aimed for around 1,000 words a day, though in his youth his target was double this and his progress was unstoppable – letters to friends include mentions of writing an 8,000-word story in two days and 55,000 words of a novel in a month.

Wodehouse (1881–1975) lived in London at 17 Dunraven Street in Mayfair from 1927 to 1934 (it now has an English Heritage Blue Plaque). In his second-floor study, now a bedroom, he wrote some of his most famous early works, including *Thank You, Jeeves* and *Very Good, Jeeves*.

But he spent the last thirty years of his life in the US, writing at his home in Remsenburg, Long Island. It was a quiet spot, the house surrounded by 12 acres (4.8 hectares) of grounds, and his writing room had large windows looking out on them. Above his

Wodehouse was a creature of habit, getting up around 7.30 a.m. every day of the week to take a walk with his dogs, followed by what he called his 'daily dozen' exercises.

desk was a Victorian oil painting of the Hongkong and Shanghai Bank's office in London where he had his first job. A recreation of this room has been set up in the library at his old school in London, Dulwich College, where he was a very happy schoolboy. On his death, his widow Ethel donated his desk, favourite Royal typewriter, pipe rack and tobacco tin to the school. Wodehouse made his own blend of pipe tobacco by crumbling cigars sent to him by his American book editor Peter Schwed.

Wodehouse was a creature of habit, getting up around 7.30 a.m. every day of the week to take a walk with his dogs,

Wodehouse made time to watch his favourite soap opera between writing sessions.

followed by what he called his 'daily dozen' exercises. These were invented by American football writer Walter Camp, who gave them vigorous names like 'grind', 'grasp' and 'curl', but were actually fairly light rather than exhausting. Then he took breakfast – toast with marmalade or honey, coffee cake and tea – during which he would usually read a book, usually detective fiction. At around 9 a.m., he went to his study to work.

If he was still in planning mode between books, he would sit in an armchair and make copious notes – these would usually number around 400 – before he began writing the new book. This could take more than a year, though he often had two books on the go at one time.

Initial work would be in pencil, followed by edits in blue or red coloured pencils. His grandson Sir Edward Cazalet still has the pencil Wodehouse was holding when he died, surrounded by rough drafts of a nearly finished new novel. Finally, he turned to the typewriter to type it up. 'I just sit at my *typewriter* and curse a bit,' is how he described his technique.

Behind the hugely popular carefree nature of his books was a tremendous amount of work. He would work very carefully on the detail of his plots to get them exactly right. While he was drafting, he would pin pages around his writing room in rows, the higher the row the happier he was with the page. Those in lower rows required more work. He knew the book was pretty much finished when all the pages were close to the picture rail.

Once he was happy, he would write up the story in considerable

detail, around 30,000 words, then return to it, working on the dialogue and fleshing it out to produce the final product.

When his morning work was done, Wodehouse would go for a walk, lunch, watch his favourite US soap opera *The Edge of Night* and then return to his study desk again from 4 p.m. to 7 p.m., finishing off the day's work in time for a cocktail, usually a stiff martini, and dinner.

He kept this routine up even during his short spell as a writer in Hollywood, with a couple of daily swims thrown in. 'The actual work is negligible,' he confided.

Writers and exercise

Sitting down in a room all day every day to write is not good for anyone's health. Novelist Haruki Murakami has likened writing a novel to survival training, and insists physical strength is as important as talent. He is a keen runner (see page 120) as is Joyce Carol Oates, who described her love of running as 'a function of writing' in her essay for the *New York Times*, 'To Invigorate Literary Mind, Start Moving Literary Feet'.

Similarly, Dan Brown says he takes brief hourly breaks during writing sessions to do stretches, sit-ups and push-ups, to keep the ideas flowing. Jack Kerouac claimed to stand on his head and then bend over to touch the floor with his toes nine times every morning.

Of course, there's nothing new in writers finding physical movement an aid to their work. Romantic poets such as William Wordsworth and Samuel Coleridge found inspiration in their walks, as did Henry David Thoreau, author of nineteenth-century nature classic *Walden*, although he disliked the description of it as exercise, saying rather that it 'is itself the enterprise and adventure of the day'. Philip Roth claimed he walked half a mile for every page he wrote. Bringing the idea into the twenty-first century are writers such as John Green (*Paper Towns, The Fault in Our Stars*), who writes using a treadmill desk.

Other writers have their own preferences, including swimming (Oliver Sacks), tennis (David Foster Wallace) and boxing (Ernest Hemingway). Science fiction author of the *Dune* prequel series Kevin J. Anderson even writes while he is hiking, speaking into a hand-held voice recorder.

Virginia Woolf
A shed of one's own

Writing shed, Rodmell, East Sussex

The 'she shed' is often regarded as a twenty-first-century concept, but the idea of a haven in the back garden to which women can retreat from the day-to-day distractions of the world – the equivalent of a 'man cave' – has a much longer history. One of the early pioneers of the 'she shed' was Virginia Woolf (1882–1941).

Woolf outlined the importance of a separate creative space for women in her short work *A Room of One's Own* (1929), arguing: 'A woman must have money and a room of her own if she is to write fiction.' In it, she maintained that historically not only had women been denied an adequate degree of financial independence and access to formal education, they had also lacked a physical space in which to write. 'In the first place, to have a room of her own, let alone a quiet room or a sound-proof room, was out of the question,' she says, 'unless her parents were exceptionally rich or very noble.' The sum Woolf estimates necessary to be financially independent is £500, which today is around £30,000, the amount the winner takes home in the UK's Women's Prize for Fiction.

At her home in Monk's House in East Sussex, Woolf had exactly such a place. The success of her novel *Orlando* allowed her to build an extension in which to write, but gradually this became her bedroom and instead she wrote mainly in a wooden shed that stood in the garden.

This writing lodge had disadvantages in that her husband Leonard used its attic to noisily sort apples from the garden and it was also too cold for writing during winter months (at which point she decamped back to the bedroom). But it was improved and moved to the end of the garden under a chestnut tree and here she sat to write, using a dip pen and ink in a low armchair with a thin piece of plywood on her lap, typing the results up later on a desk. She particularly liked using blue writing paper.

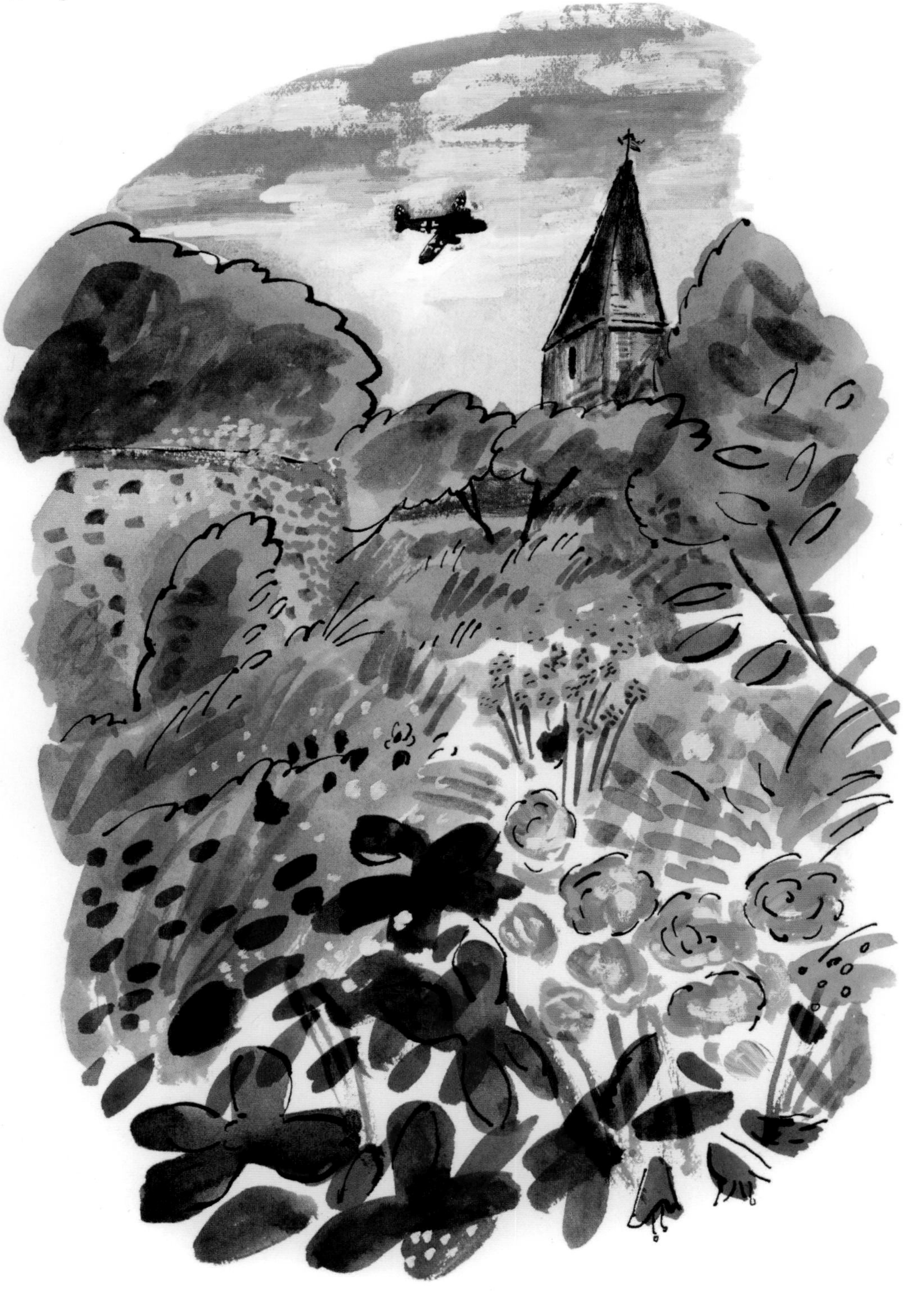

Woolf's friend Lytton Strachey complained that she surrounded herself with 'filth packets' as she wrote: cigarette ends, pen nibs and various bits of paper. Over her lifetime she also had several tables or desks, including one standing desk. Annie Leibovitz photographed the top of her table in the writing lodge for her book *Pilgrimage* and this clearly shows the surface is scarred with plenty of mug rings and spilt ink.

Through the window, Woolf had views towards the Sussex Downs and Mount Caburn. The lodge also had a brick seating area in front of it on which she and friends and family would sit and watch games of bowls on the lawn with the Sussex Downs as a backdrop. During the Second World War, German planes flew low over their home. 'Bombs shook the window of my lodge,' she wrote, another echo of *A Room of One's Own*, which also discusses women living in dangerous surroundings. It was here that she produced *Mrs Dalloway*, *The Waves* and *Between the Acts*.

'We should have felt it to be not merely wrong but unpleasant not to work every morning for seven days a week and for about eleven months of the year.'

She wrote mainly in the mornings. Leonard describes her walking out to work at the writing lodge 'with the regularity of a stockbroker'. In a letter to her lover Vita Sackville-West, she describes this commute: 'I wake filled with a tremulous yet steady rapture, carry my pitcher full of lucid and deep water across the garden.' In another letter, to her friend Ethel Smyth, she wrote: '[I] shall smell a red rose; shall gently surge across the lawn (I move as if I carried a basket of eggs on my head) light a cigarette, take my writing board on my knee; and let myself down, like a diver, very cautiously into the last sentence I wrote yesterday.'

Leonard also points out that his wife maintained a strict schedule. 'We should have felt it to be not merely wrong but unpleasant not to work every morning for seven days a week and for about eleven months of the year,' he wrote. 'Every morning, therefore, at about 9.30 after breakfast, each of us, as if moved by a law of unquestioned nature, went off and worked until lunch at 1.' On warm days in the summer, she would also sleep there.

William Wordsworth
A moss hut with a view

Writing hut, Grasmere, Lake District, Cumbria

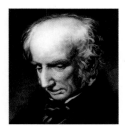

When English poet William Wordsworth (1770–1850) and his sister Dorothy took a tour of Scotland in 1803, they came across a building Dorothy described as a 'hay-stack scooped out'. It was a simple circular, domed wooden hut, lined with moss.

As soon as they got back to their Dove Cottage home in the Lake District, William and Dorothy set about building their own version. But as Dorothy noted in her travelogue 'Recollections of a Tour Made in Scotland', it was sited in the wrong place. 'We wished we could have shoved it about a hundred yards further on,' she wrote, to have finer views and be more secluded from walkers.

By the autumn of 1804, the new hut was in place, at the top of their garden, and higher than the cottage. While Wordsworth wrote in most of the rooms of his home, this was where he was happiest working. It was lined with moss and covered outside with heather, with a long seat around the interior. William likened it to a wren's nest, facing west for the afternoon sun.

It was Wordsworth's retreat from the world in general and the noisy atmosphere of the cottage – he described it as his 'charming little temple' to his brother. He had a short but steep climb up stone steps to get to the hut, which emphasized the feeling of remoteness but still allowed him to connect his life and his home with the natural surroundings. The working conditions were certainly inspirational, as it was during this time that he wrote some of his most famous poems, including *The Prelude* and 'I Wandered Lonely as a Cloud'.

After the siblings left the house, the new owner demolished the moss hut. But Wordsworth loved his moss writing room so much that he built another modest stone writing hut at his next (much larger) home at nearby Rydal Mount. Here, a servant once told a visitor that while Wordsworth kept his books in his library, 'his study is out of doors'.

Wordsworth's lost moss hut was replaced in 2020 with a new one built out of Cumbrian oak, along the same nest-like lines as the original.

'Make them laugh, make them cry, make them wait.'

Charles Dickens

'People bother me.
I come here to hide
from them.'

George Bernard Shaw

Visitor information

Many of the locations described in this book are private, and cannot be visited.

W.H. Auden

Visits to the Auden museum are on weekdays by appointment only. www.kirchstetten.at/unser_kirchstetten/audenhaus

Jane Austen

The Steventon rectory, where Jane Austen wrote her early work, was demolished in 1824, though a lime tree supposedly planted in 1813 by her brother James marks the spot where it stood. Austen's Grade I listed Chawton Cottage home now also contains the Jane Austen's House Museum (www.janeaustens.house) where you can see her writing table in the dining parlour. The author's writing box is on display at the Sir John Ritblat Gallery at the British Library in London (www.bl.uk).

James Baldwin

James Baldwin's house no longer exists and there is no memorial to him in Saint-Paul de Vence, although La Colombe d'Or Hotel and Café de la Place which he often frequented can still be visited. More details at www.saint-pauldevence.com/en

Honoré de Balzac

The Maison de Balzac (www.maisondebalzac.paris.fr, also available in English) also has a permanent display of Balzac's manuscripts. Musée Balzac: www.lysdanslavallee.fr/en/contenu/balzac-museum

Ray Bradbury

Bradbury's home has been demolished, but the Center for Ray Bradbury Studies at the Indiana University–Purdue University Indianapolis has a huge archive of Bradbury's work and writings. It has also recreated his basement office with Bradbury's original writing desk, typewriters, paintbox, bookcases and chairs. https://bradbury.iupui.edu/

The Brontës

The Brontë Parsonage Museum (www.bronte.org.uk) is in Haworth, West Yorkshire.

Anton Chekhov

You can visit Chekhov's home in Melikhovo (http://en.chekhovmuseum.com), the White Dacha, now a writer's museum (http://yalta-museum.ru/ru/dom-muzej-ap-chehova-v-jalte.html – in Russian), and his house museum in Moscow (www.goslitmuz.ru/museums/dom-muzey-a-p-chekhova – in Russian) .

Agatha Christie

Most of Christie's houses are now private residences but Greenway is open to the public through the National Trust. www.nationaltrust.org.uk/greenway. Room 411 at the Pera Palace in Turkey is available to book. www.perapalace.com/en-US/room-type/281721

Colette

Colette's birthplace and childhood homes are in Burgundy's Saint-Sauveur-en-Puisaye in France (www.maisondecolette.fr and www.musee-colette.com). Her Paris flat is not open to the public and her country house at 41 chemin des Montboucons in Besançon (where there is a museum dedicated to Victor Hugo who was born in the town) in the Doubs department is privately owned, though does open very occasionally.

Roald Dahl

The interior of Dahl's writing hut was moved into the Roald Dahl Museum and Story Centre in Great Missenden in 2012. www.roalddahl.com/museum

Charles Dickens

Tavistock House was demolished in 1901 although a Blue Plaque marks the spot. Gad's Hill is now the home of Gad's Hill School – monthly tours can be booked via Visit Gravesend (www.visitgravesend.co.uk). The Charles Dickens Museum is at 48 Doughty Street (www.dickensmuseum.com) and is open weekdays (except Mondays) with regular tours and exhibitions. The writing chalet has since been moved to Eastgate House in Rochester's High Street, although it is in a poor state of repair and fundraising activities for conservation works are ongoing.

Emily Dickinson

The Emily Dickinson Museum, 280 Main Street, Amherst MA 01002. www.emilydickinsonmuseum.org

Arthur Conan Doyle

Conan Doyle's home at 12 Tennison Road, South Norwood is private, but a Blue Plaque recognizes his time there. Stonyhurst is open to the public on specific days during school holidays. www.stonyhurst.ac.uk/open-to-the-public/historic-collections-archives-and-museum/visit

Ian Fleming

Goldeneye, now much renovated and updated, is available for rent. Visitors can sit at Fleming's desk and chair which are still in situ. www.theflemingvilla.com

Thomas Hardy

The National Trust owns what is now known as Hardy's Cottage as well as Max Gate, the larger home he moved to in nearby Dorchester (www.nationaltrust.org.uk/hardys-cottage and www.nationaltrust.org.uk/max-gate). A replica of his study there, where he continued to write, is also on display in the town's Dorset County Museum. www.dorsetcountymuseum.org

Ernest Hemingway

The Finca Vigía is open to the public and remains virtually unchanged since Hemingway left it in 1960 (not realizing that he would never return). https://en.hemingwayhavana.com. You can also peer into Hemingway's writing room at the carriage house at his previous home in Key West, Florida, now the Ernest Hemingway Home and Museum. Unfortunately, it is behind a plexiglass barrier and you cannot cross the threshold. www.hemingwayhome.com

Victor Hugo

After extensive restoration work, Hauteville House and the Lookout opened again to the public in 2019. www.maisonsvictorhugo.paris.fr/en/museum-collections/house-visit-guernsey

Samuel Johnson

Dr Johnson's House (www.drjohnsonshouse.org) is open to the public and has a careful curation policy so that it is not filled with objects unconnected to the writer. Its permanent collection includes forty of his manuscripts and Johnson's walking stick and letter case.

Stephen King

This is a private home, though there are plans to turn King's house in Bangor, Maine, into a residential retreat for writers and a home for his archives.

Rudyard Kipling

Naulakah is available to rent from the Landmark Trust USA (sleeps eight), enabling you to sit at Kipling's desk, since much of the original furniture is still on site. https://landmarktrustusa.org/rudyard-kiplings-naulakha
Bateman's is run by the National Trust and the study is open to visitors. www.nationaltrust.org.uk/batemans

D.H. Lawrence

D.H. Lawrence Ranch is open to the public, although with limited visiting times. Lawrence's tree is still standing. https://dhlawrenceranch.unm.edu. It is possible to rent the Villa Mirenda, now known as Lawrence's House, via major booking portals.

Astrid Lindgren

Astrid Lindgren's home is at Dalagatan 46, Stockholm, and is open via guided tours in Swedish and sometimes in English. Tickets must be booked in advance but strangely children under fifteen are not allowed in. Details at www.astridlindgren.com/en (where there is an excellent 360-degree virtual tour of the flat).

Jack London

You can visit the stone ruins of Wolf House in the Jack London State Historic Park (www.jacklondonpark.com) as well as London's cottage and writing room. There is also a visitor centre and museum to his memory as well as his grave.

Margaret Mitchell

The Margaret Mitchell House and Museum (www.atlantahistorycenter.com/buildings-and-grounds/atlanta-history-center-midtown) is in central Atlanta. As well as visiting the room where Mitchell wrote, its exhibitions look at the issues covered in the book. The city's Atlanta Fulton County Central Library has a special Margaret Mitchell Collection, including the typewriter she used to write *Gone With the Wind*, her Pulitzer Prize, photos, library card and personal book library.

Michel de Montaigne

Montaigne's tower happily survived a huge fire in the late nineteenth century. It can be visited, and although his library and shelving have gone, the beam quotations are still visible. www.chateau-montaigne.com/en

George Orwell

Barnhill, still extremely secluded, is available to rent. www.escapetojura.com/Barnhill.html

Sylvia Plath

Plath's homes in America and England, including Court Green, are private residences. There is a Blue Plaque commemorating her life at 3 Chalcot Square in London, where she lived and worked with Ted Hughes from January 1960 to August 1961. Her home at 23 Fitzroy Road has a Blue Plaque for W.B. Yeats, set up several years before she moved there.

Beatrix Potter

Hill Top is owned and run by the National Trust. www.nationaltrust.org.uk/hill-top. Castle Cottage is now available to rent.

Marcel Proust
Proust's original apartment at 102 Boulevard Haussmann is now a bank, but his bedroom at his next (and last) home in Rue Hamelin been recreated at the city's Musée Carnavalet (www.carnavalet.paris.fr) as a permanent exhibit, as has that of Anna de Noailles.

J.K. Rowling
Spoon (www.spoonedinburgh.co.uk) and the Elephant House (www.elephanthouse.biz) are both in Edinburgh.

Vita Sackville-West
Sissinghurst is owned by the National Trust. www.nationaltrust.org.uk/sissinghurst-castle-garden. The gazebo is open to the public but visitors can only look into Vita's writing space from behind a barrier. In another room in the tower is the cast-iron Cropper Minerva platen printing press, which Virginia Woolf and her husband Leonard used at their Hogarth Press publishing house. It was used to print some of Vita's own books as well as the first UK edition of T.S. Eliot's *The Waste Land* (1923). A present from the Woolfs, Vita used it to print work including her poem 'Sissinghurst'.

George Bernard Shaw
Shaw's Corner is owned by the National Trust. www.nationaltrust.org.uk/shaws-corner

Gertrude Stein
Stein's home in Paris where she and Toklas held their salons is at 27 Rue de Fleurus. It's a private property but a plaque outside commemorates her time there.

John Steinbeck
The properties at Sag Harbor and New York are private, but Steinbeck also wrote *The Log from the Sea of Cortez* in a small shedlike building in Pacific Grove, California, which is available to rent on Airbnb www.airbnb.co.uk/rooms/1325979.

Dylan Thomas
The Boathouse (www.dylanthomasboathouse.com) now contains a museum dedicated to Thomas. Visitors can peek into the shed but it is closed to the public. The shed's original doors were rescued from a council rubbish tip in the 1970s and are on display with other Thomas memorabilia in the Dylan Thomas Centre in Swansea (www.dylanthomas.com).

Mark Twain
In 1952, the writing shed was moved to the campus of Elmira College in 1952, home to the Center for Mark Twain Studies, and is free to visit during the summer (Memorial Day to Labor Day. www.marktwainstudies.com. The house in Hartford is also open to the public, who can book three-hour sessions to write (pencils only, no pens) in the bookshelf-lined library. marktwainhouse.org

Kurt Vonnegut
Kurt Vonnegut Museum and Library. www.vonnegutlibrary.org. The Lilly Library at the nearby Indiana University holds the main archive of Vonnegut's letters, papers and manuscripts including the stapled scrolls which are stored rolled up (www.libraries.indiana.edu/lilly-library).

Edith Wharton
After various post-Wharton incarnations, including as a girls' school dormitory and theatre space, the Mount (www.edithwharton.org) and its gardens are open to the public and have undergone a series of major restorations in recent decades, including major work on the bedroom suite.

P.G. Wodehouse
Wodehouse's home in Long Island is a private residence. The recreated writing room at Dulwich College (www.dulwich.org.uk) can be viewed by prior appointment.

Virginia Woolf
Monk's House, in Lewes, East Sussex, is open for pre-booked visits from April to November. www.nationaltrust.org.uk/monks-house

William Wordsworth
Both Dove Cottage (www.wordsworth.org.uk) and Rydal Mount are now writers' home museums and open to the public (www.rydalmount.co.uk).

Index

Picture credits

To Phyllis and Philip, Wilma,
Robert, Edward and Thomas

First published in 2022
by Frances Lincoln,
an imprint of The Quarto Group.
The Old Brewery, 6 Blundell Street,
London, N7 9BH, United Kingdom
(0)20 7700 6700
www.Quarto.com

Front cover illustration:
Sylvia Plath's writing room at Court Green,
in North Tawton, Devon

ISBN 978-0-7112-5801-3
Ebook ISBN 978-0-7112-5803-7

10 9 8 7 6 5 4 3 2 1

Design by Glenn Howard/Untitled
Printed in China

Inspiring | Educating | Creating | Entertaining